THE FOUR CAPITALS FOR SUCCESS:

A Personal Leadership Guide

GOSKI ALABI, PhD

authorHOUSE

AuthorHouse™
1663 Liberty Drive
Bloomington, IN 47403
www.authorhouse.com
Phone: 833-262-8899

Published by AuthorHouse 04/22/2022

ISBN: 978-1-6655-4626-3 (sc)
ISBN: 978-1-6655-4636-2 (e)

Print information available on the last page.

Any people depicted in stock imagery provided by Getty Images are models, and such images are being used for illustrative purposes only.
Certain stock imagery © Getty Images.

This book is printed on acid-free paper.

CONTENTS

PREFACE

There is no 'Formula for Success'. Everybody's life has its own purpose, destination and timing, therefore, no particular path or set of actions should be prescribed for success in life. Some people succeed while others fail. However, successful people do share some skills and abilities in common. This begs the question; what are these traits that successful people have, and can everyone who learns the secrets of success and applies the needed skills and abilities succeed? Some people believe that certain people are destined for success or accomplishments while others are destined to remain unaccomplished. Others believe that success is gained through luck. Others still, believe success is based on a combination of factors which include knowledge gained through experience, how you use this knowledge combined with the information you have at a given time, how hard you work, luck, faith or fate. Some say good luck counts, but not without the bad because the bad propels some people to greater heights. The question remains, how do people become successful?

People often get scholarships to the best schools, not simply as a result of academic aptitude, but their 'unlucky' socio-economic status may offer them opportunities that equally qualified candidates don't have. There are people who got terrific job offers because one interview question landed them an offer. Have you ever heard of people who were rejected by a university only to end up employing graduates from those same universities, and giving graduation speeches at those same university? Jack Ma, for example. What made the difference for him when the tides were initially against him, and how do other people overcome these hurdles? People like Einstein and Thomas Edison, who were deemed poor students at school, ended up changing the world with their inventions There are billionaires impacting the world now who grew up in very poor homes and poor communities. It's often true that rich families become richer and maintain their social status for generations, but this doesn't mean that their economic status isn't achievable to those who aren't born into such a family. The question is what sets people like Elon Mask, Bill Gates, Steve Jobs, Richard Branson, Nelson Mandela, Kwame Nkrumah and Oprah Winfrey apart?

This question leaves us with many more questions. Are these coincidental or accidental encounters, that is to say, are these opportunities forced from a particular outlook on life, or are such encounters based on some principles of natural exclusivity, or based on intentionality? Where does being intentional about personal growth and accomplishment fit in the equation of success in life? What at all is success, and what is the yardstick for measuring success in life? Should success be a goal that is to be chased?

This book explores these questions and provides some insights based on careful considerations and examples of practices employed by people commonly perceived to be successful. No set can determine the equation of success, but success can be guided. This book therefore focuses on the conscious part of success and emphasizes the skills and abilities that successful people share. It lays the foundation for personal leadership and discusses some of the tensions associated with the subject of success.

The 4 Capitals for Success and Guide for Personal Leadership provides some insights for success based on practical life examples. Using reviews and insights from highly recommended books that have transformed lives, the 4 Capitals of Success, catalogues skills, principles, and practices that can bring meaning and success to your personal life. The 4 Capitals is indeed full of everyday examples that can bring improvement and fulfilment to your life no matter where you are.

The book discusses views on personal leadership, the various personality quotients, and how they each contribute to personal success and meaning in life; the role of Fate, Faith, Work and Luck; nature versus nurturing, 'The Way, and Knowing the Right way'; the key factors that limit self-development and the power of thoughts and actions in the pursuit of success. Finally, this book offers a guide on how you can develop and deploy the 4 Capitals to make a difference. The book is in two Parts. Part one covers Principles of Personal Leadership and Part 2 the Four Capitals.

No matter, where you are in life and what you are doing, the 4 Capitals can make a difference and bring enrichment and fulfilment to your life.

PRINCIPLES OF PERSONAL LEADERSHIP

CHAPTER 1

PERSONAL LEADERSHIP

*Deep within humans dwell those slumbering powers; powers that would
astonish them, that they never dreamed of possessing; forces that would
revolutionize their lives if aroused and put into action. - Orison Marden*

INTRODUCTION

Personal leadership is the foundation of all other leadership abilities and
personal success. Those who cannot lead themselves cannot lead a group,
a team, a nation, or a continent. However, leading oneself requires a set of
skills and abilities. Key personal leadership skills that have been advocated
over time include *self-awareness, awareness of others, self-direction, self-
regulation, self-control* and *self-development*. The possession of these skills
and other requisite abilities are part of the four capitals for success.

Success has been defined as the accomplishment of an aim or purpose.
Here, whether positive or negative, once an aim is accomplished, one can
be considered to be successful. Aims are determined by people themselves.
On the other hand, everybody's purpose in life is different, and so is the
opportunity to fulfil that purpose. Each of us is created for a purpose and if
we fulfil our purpose, we are successful. When our aim is derived from our
purpose, then we can be both accomplished and fulfilled. However, when
your aim is not aligned to your purpose, but you achieve your aim, you
may be accomplished but not fulfilled. There are many real-life examples

of people who were accomplished but not fulfilled. An example is Pablo Escobar, the columbium drug lord who become the 7th richest man on earth but died a day after his 42nd birthday in a manhunt as a fugitive[1]. His story is discussed in more detail later in this book.

The challenge for most people is identifying their purpose in life. Only then can we fulfil it and be successful. Success, in my opinion, is the positive impact of the fulfilment of our purpose in life, not the mere accomplishment of aims.

Personal leadership is the foundation of personal success. Yet, thriving for success goes beyond the traditional notion of personal leadership. The miraculous survival and continuous efforts of the young and heroic Malala is an example of this. She spoke out against the Taliban's ban on girls going to school in Pakistan in 2011 and was shot for her beliefs. She said, "I had two options: to remain salient and wait to be killed, and the second was to speak up and then be killed. I chose the second. They thought the bullet would silence us, but they failed. They could shoot my head, but not my dreams, my vision."[2] Malala had to thrive to be successful. What if Malala had not survived, would she have been successful? Malala's story is also discussed later on in this book.

Malala's story reaffirms the importance of personal leadership for success. Malala was clear about her purpose in life. She found purpose in her voice, her oratorical gift, and believed that she had to be a voice for the 6.6 million girls who could not have access to school. Not even a bullet could silence her. She knew that to fulfil her purpose, she must aim at going to school and getting a good education but her prize did not come without a price and some perils.

Fulfilling your purpose in life is all what success in life is all about. But, as mentioned above, everyone's life purpose is different, and their opportunity to make it happen is also unique. No particular path or set of actions can be prescribed for success, because everyone's circumstances

---

[1]   Forbes, 2013, https://www.forbes.com/sites/doliaestevez/2013/10/01/was-mexican-fugitive-caro-quintero-the-first-billionaire-drug-lord/?sh=297a1656abcf, retrieved May 11, 2021

[2]   New York Times, 2013, The making of Malala Yousafzai, Story of the Girl Shot in Taliban Attack. October 7th 2013, https://www.youtube.com/watch?v=AitiZ8nTabM, Retrieved May 11, 2021

and calling are different. If people's purpose, paths and destinations are different, why should we use a common yardstick to measure how successful people are? Although everyone has their individual journey to success, we can learn from sharing principles and practices that have worked for many successful people. This guide offers many of these examples and begins with the principles of personal leadership.

To discover your purpose in life, you should ask yourselves: what was I created for? Why do I exist, what do I exist to do, and what values and actions can help me fulfil my purpose? The answers to these questions should set the tone for defining your personal leadership profile. Purpose, meaning in life, and values, are the foundation of personal leadership. So, what is your purpose in life? What are you living for? What do you exist to do for humanity? What do you value in life, and why do you value those things or principles? The value systems of our environment and our own value systems define how we lead our lives.

*

When you live in a society that values money or riches over contribution to human welfare, you may see nothing wrong with getting rich at any expense. You may even be tempted to use rituals for money, after all, the end justifies the means, process is not important. It takes something else to be different in such circumstances. On the other hand, if you live in a community that celebrates contribution, you are likely to channel your energies in that direction. But what if I told you both of them are your choice? You choose what to live for and what to value in life. The will to choose your own way and how you make a difference is something that cannot be easily taken away from you.

Personal leadership has to do with the ability to make a difference with one's life. It is about finding meaning and fulfilling destiny in a way that touches other lives. That is what I call making a life, not a living. Those who make a living often make no significant difference, whereas those who make a life leave their marks in time. There is a big difference between making a life and making a living. As Winston Churchill said,

"We make a living by what we get, but we make a life by what we give."[3] What are you giving to the world, your country, your community and society in general? Personal leadership is about making a life not a living. The following chapters present the principles of personal leadership.

---

[3] Winston Churchill, https://www.quora.com/We-make-a-living-by-what-we-get-We-make-a-life-by-what-we-give-What-does-this-mean-and-lead-to, Retrieved April, 20, 2019.

CHAPTER 2

PERSONAL LEADERSHIP PRINCIPLE 1: KNOW YOURSELF

KNOWING YOURSELF AS A PERSON: SELF-AWARENESS AND AWARENESS OF OTHERS

It is important to understand that you are unique, that no one else can be you, and that your life can never be replaced or repeated. If you are not aware of yourself, who you are, and what makes you unique, then any wind can blow you in any direction, because the roots holding you up are not firm. If you are self-aware, then you know your Purpose, Passion, Strengths and Weaknesses, the Opportunities you have, and the unique Challenges in your life. You also will know the values that make you fulfilled, which enables you to direct and regulate yourself. To get the best out of yourself and your life, you must know who you are. What works for you and what does not work for you. There are foods that work for you, but may not work for others, and those that work for others, may not work for you. The creams that work for others may not work for you, or even work differently for you because your blood type and genetic makeup is so distinct. The things that get on your nerves may bring happiness to others, simply because your personality is different and distinct. The point is we're all different. You cannot be everything to everybody. You have a specific assignment in life, and it is your obligation to carry it out if you want to find success.

However, personal leadership requires a set of leadership skills that are different from the skills required at all other levels of leadership. This set of skills and tools can help you understand yourself and others and make the best out of your life. These include:

- **Intrapersonal skills** (which include intelligence quotient [IQ], emotional intelligence quotient [EQ], adversity quotient [AQ]. This I call your **Personal Capital**
- **Interhuman Skills:** This refers to what you can put at the disposal of others to make life better or easier for them. It includes your Knowledge and your Skills. This is what I call your **Human Capital**.
- **Interpersonal Skills:** This refers to your relational skills, that is team or group skills and networking skills; social intelligence (SQ). I call this **Social Capital**.
- **Extra personal Skills:** These are what give us the ability to transcend self-interest, uphold the common good, practice good citizenship behaviour, and to have confidence in whatever we set out to do, irrespective of the obstacles or challenges that may come our way. (Spiritual Skills). This I call **Spiritual Capital**.

These are the 4 capitals that we need for personal leadership. Success and fulfilment therefore require Personal Capital, Human Capital, Social Capital and Spiritual Capital. We will explore these in more detail in part 2 of this book.

CHAPTER 3

PERSONAL LEADERSHIP PRINCIPLE 2: SELF-DIRECTION

Where there is no destination, any road can lead anywhere[4].

Self-direction refers to setting personal goals and defining aspirations, then motivating yourself to accomplish those goals and aspirations. This requires you to identify your purpose, your calling or vocation, your personal interests, and your passion and drives. *Purpose and passion* are the key driving forces of positive self-direction. Passion without purpose is desire for nothing, and purpose without passion is a dead desire. Many of us find ourselves pursuing other people's dreams and living other people's lives and aspirations because we feel that is what is expected of us.

To locate your purpose and your passion, try to identify things you do with ease, and things that others commend you for (these are your talents). But talents must be polished and turned into abilities for the needed impact. Finding answers to the statements below can help you locate your purpose and passion

- o People always tell me am good at...........
- o I feel very fulfilled when I ....
- o I have a talent for ....
- o I have nurtured my talent so I can ....

---

4   A personal quote I developed while writing this book. Similar to Lewis Carroll Quote but quite different "If you don't know where you are going, any road will get you there".

7

- ○ I love to do the following and I do it with ease ....
- ○ I am doing what I love most, and I make a living from that....

What is the difference between what you currently do, your talent, skills, abilities, and what you aspire to?

Talent alone is not enough. Talent is like a precious mineral that needs to be unearthed and polished or refined to have more value. Talent may not be abilities, but in our talents lie our abilities (both known and unknown to us) and our latent drives. Once we discover our talents, we can turn them into abilities and drives.

Identify something that naturally makes you happy and lights you up. Anything that often takes away from your joy, or things you do only with difficulty, may not be your passion. Your purpose may not be aligned to those things. To identify your passion and drives, ask yourself the following questions:

- When I was a child, what did I dream of doing?
- What changed and why?

Remember, passion is the driving force for self-direction. Where there is a will, there is a way. Look at your past and note any significant changes and successes. You need some milestones to remind you of where you are going and where you should be going. I know a lot of professionals who hate their jobs, yet they are stuck in them because they do not know how to get out. Identifying the things that bring you joy and which you do with relative ease will help you find your way to the next milestone, which is aligned to your purpose. If you do not have any goals developed for yourself for the next five to ten years, then it is time to develop some, write them down, and post them in a place where you will see them every day. The way you want to see yourself in 5-10 years from now is your **Personal Vision,** and it should be derived from your Purpose and Passion.

LOCATING MY PURPOSE AND PASSION IN LIFE: A PERSONAL EXAMPLE

I was born in a small town called Nungua in the Greater Accra Region of Ghana in April 1970. During my primary school age, I lived with my grandparents, who were artisans in the midst of fishmongers. My community did not value an academic education highly, and so many children, particularly girls, did not take to education in general. While I was growing up, my father pushed the idea that a university education was everything that a person needed to succeed and break the cycle of abject poverty. This idea took such a hold of me that my only aspiration in life was to be a university graduate. It did not matter what profession, program, or qualification; all I needed was a university degree. So I started learning about what it would take for me to get there.

In my mind, without a university education, I would be nothing, and no one would see what I had to offer. By the age of six or seven, I had started nurturing these thoughts. By the time I was twelve, my father, a civil engineer by profession, had already directed my mind toward the sciences, and rightly so, because I had a great desire for a university education, but nothing in particular to hope for.

For me, there is no doubt that when a land is fertile and prepared, anything can be grown on it, good or bad, even weeds. The state I was in exemplified desire (*passion) without purpose.*

Until then, my only intentions were to enter university, but for what? Nothing. At the time, I was about to enter high school, I believed that only the brilliant and academically outstanding studied science. In fact, Ghanaian society had precipitated and fuelled this perception, and this was coupled with an overwhelming gender bias against females. I was determined to prove to my community that what a man can do, a woman can do equally well. This was my father's dream, because at this time he had only female children. I had to live my father's dreams and aspirations. To encourage me and further solidify the precipitated passion, he got me a newspaper article about Margaret Thatcher. I learnt through that article that she read Chemistry at university and later became a lawyer. That was my example to follow, but to follow for what and to where?

I found out later, I am not a scientist. I studied science in secondary school, read physics, chemistry, and mathematics at A level, and earned a B.Sc. in Chemistry and an M.Phil in Food science, only to discover that I had been living my father's, and society's, dreams – not mine. I am a chemist by training, but not a chemist by passion. By passion, I am a speaker and an advocate, and someone interested in shaping policy and practice through my knowledge.

I thank God that I recognized and decided to follow my passion to become a teacher. Now I speak and write for a living, and in doing so I am able to make a life, not just a living. I recall, one day someone I met at my children's school asked me what I did for a living. With a smile, I responded, "I am a teacher." One of my very good friends who was there with me at the time turned and walked away. Once the person who had asked the question left, my friend came back and said to me, "Why did you introduce yourself as a teacher? You know how teachers are perceived here. Trust me, they won't treat your children with respect and dignity." So I asked her, "What did you expect me to say? I *am* a teacher, and I love it. It doesn't matter how others perceive it. Being a teacher is what I'm called to be. I'm not ashamed to be one."

Ironically, my friend was a teacher too, in the same school where I had my children, but she did not want anyone outside her workplace to know that she was a teacher. She always looked forward to the end of the workday in anticipation of a better life somewhere out there. She believed that one day she would land a job that would make her truly happy. Does this friend have the calling to be a teacher? Maybe yes, maybe no.

Going through my personal development plan and profile, I realized that I was as young as eight years old when I started doing what a Jehovah's Witnesses calls "speaking assignments" in the congregation that my family belonged to. Each time I had an assignment, the hall was full of people. Both adults and children loved to listen to me on stage. I presented my assignments with such passion and joy that people would always commend me at the end. My voice added to my gift and talent for speaking, but I needed to develop and hone my speaking abilities. Naturally, I loved listening to great public speakers, and I practised a lot in my mind's eye. I would normally see myself speaking to an imaginary audience. I enjoyed those soul-level expeditions. I looked forward to any time I had an assignment. I learned early enough that *talent is not enough, ability is required, so talent should be developed into a reliable ability.*

I had a talent for speaking in public, but no one spotted and nurtured it. I had to be a scientist to please my father and society, but that was not my calling. Today, speaking around the world comes to me naturally, because that is what I am called to do, and I developed and nurtured that talent into an ability. It is my vocation, and that seed was in me from birth. It is through speaking that I make my difference.

Steve Jobs admonishes, "Your time is limited, so don't waste it living someone else's life. Don't be trapped by dogma, which is living with the results of other people's thinking. Don't let the noise of others' opinions drown out your own inner voice. And most importantly, have the courage to follow your heart and intuition. They somehow already know what you truly want to become. Everything else is secondary."

What is your calling? Are you living other people's dreams? Locate your talent, passion, and purpose in life by taking a personal development test using the GAB questionnaire provided in Appendix A.

CHAPTER 4

PERSONAL LEADERSHIP PRINCIPLE 3: SELF-REGULATION AND SELF-CONTROL

Anyone who cannot control and regulate him/herself is like a candle in the wind. Any wind can blow such a person in any direction and thereby cause him/her to lose focus. Someone once said to me, "Don't mind that fellow—he has no spine of his own." I asked, "Why?" The individual replied, "You can tune him around the clock. Anyone at all can convince him to do one thing or the other; he has no values to live by." Do you have a backbone?

Self-control is the ability to do that which you ought to do and refraining from that which you ought not to do. Self-control is self-discipline. Self-control is what stops the guilty mind from manifesting. Self-control is our ability to say no when we need to, or to walk away from potential threats or trouble. Self-control is how we are able to put our emotions in check and hold our mouths from speaking evil[5]. Self-control has also been defined as the ability to delay immediate gratification of a smaller reward for a larger reward later in time and a long-term option with a larger reward value [6].

---

[5] Stuart Shanker D.Phil. 2016, Self-Regulation vs. Self-Control the reason for the profound differences lies deep inside the brain. Psychology Today, https://www.psychologytoday.com/us/blog/self-reg/201607/self-regulation-vs-self-control, retrieved May 23rd, 2021

[6] (Ainslie, 1975; Mischel et al. 1989; Kirby and Herrnstein, 1995).

Self-regulation on the other hand is our ability to monitor our behaviors, thoughts and emotions, so that we can control ourselves or put ourselves in check. Self-regulation therefore requires stopping from time to time to check ourselves and introspect to see whether we are living our values, purpose, and passion, or whether what you are doing works and if not, making the necessary changes for personal correction and improvement.

This means self-regulation is possible when we learn. We therefore need personal standards of behaviors called personal values and principle against which to regulate ourselves. When something is acceptable to you and you do not see anything wrong with it, you may not be able to regulate yourself against it. You must accept that something is not what you want and does not work for you to be able to regulate yourself against it. Self-regulation is therefore required for self-control to be effective.

Stuart Shanker defines self-control as the ability to inhibit strong impulses, while self-regulation is about reducing the rate and amount of strong impulses by managing stress-load and recovery through learning. According to Shanker, from a scientific and psychological point of view, self-regulation is what makes self-control possible, or in some instances needless. The reason he argues, lies deep inside the brain. According to him, when they looked into the images of highly provoked children's brains in a research, they observed that the limbic system, which is the source of strong emotions and impulses, were more activated, lit up in bright shades of red, while there were only a few splashes of blue in the prefrontal cortex (PFC), the seat of our rational and reflective selves is taking a back seat. This situation reverses when the children were calmed down. Once the limbic system is activated, it can drive appetites and impulses.

This observation suggests that calm turns the "limbic alarm" off, which makes the brain quickly shift from a "survival-defensive mode" to "learning mode making self-regulation possible." This implies that the systems used to think about one's actions are related to pre-frontal cortex. According to Plato for self-control to be possible, Reason must rein in appetites and impulses. Therefore, to regulate oneself, one can take a deep breath and calm down so that reason can rein.

Self-control relates more to the consequences of poor behavioural tendencies. Self-control therefore demands more reflection before actions when our appetites and impulses get in the way. Thankfully, we can develop self-control through emotional intelligence. To illustrate this, think about a time when you were emotionally worked up. Were you receptive to criticism or even constructive advice? Of course not. However, Shanker observes that becoming self-aware allows for self-regulation, and in turn, makes self-control possible. Practically when our appetites, impulses and drives get in the way, we need to take a moment, through a deep breath or a blink or by just closing our eyes to imagine our calm state to shift the brain to the Pre-frontal cortex which will the allow us to calm down.

IMPORTANCE OF SELF CONTROL FOR PERSONAL LEADERSHIP AND SUCCESS

The significance of self-control for behaviour, well-being, and personal success is unquestionable. Self-control and regulation allow for the needed discipline to do what is expected of us and avoid unnecessary distractions that may deprive us of reaching our personal goals and fulfilling our purpose.

In a perspective article published by Frontiers in Psychology in July 2018, Marleen Gillebaart noted that numerous studies provide evidence that the level of self-control at a young age can predict cognitive and self-regulatory skills in adolescence.[7] This suggests that training children how to develop their emotional intelligence can help the individual master self-control and regulation. In addition, Moffitt and colleagues (2011) report that self-control is related to crucial personal outcomes like health and well-being later in life. Tangney and others also reported a relationship between self-control and academic achievements,[8] better quality interpersonal relationships,[9] and basically, a happier life.[10] Inversely, being prone to low self-control is associated with problematic behaviours and outcomes such as impulse buying[11] and financial debt,[12] maladaptive eating patterns

---

[7]   (Shoda et al. 1990).

[8]   (Tangney et al., 2004; Duckworth and Seligman, 2005),

[9]   (Vohs et al., 2011

[10]   (Cheung et al., 2014; Hofmann et al., 2014

[11]   (Baumeister, 2002)

[12]   (Gathergood, 2012),

(Elfhag and Morey, 2008), and procrastination (Tice and Baumeister, 1997). Owing to the strong associations between self-control and the countless behavioural outcomes, self-control has been coined a 'hallmark of adaptation'.[13] This makes self-control and regulation an important ingredient for personal leadership and success.

Self-regulation and control require respect for oneself, one's values, and one's space, and respect for others. It also requires respect for systems and environmental regulation. Personal integrity and discipline, which is, keeping one's promises, refraining from that which ought not to be done, and doing what ought to be done at the right time and in the most prudent way, is also required.

ELEMENTS FOR SELF-REGULATION

Marleen further identified three main ingredients of self-regulation: *standards, monitoring, and operating.* According to Marleen, "to self-regulate successfully, there needs to be a desired end or standard identified by the individual. Without such a standard, there is no direction for self-regulation, and also no motivation to steer or alter any behaviour in a specific direction. Additionally, in order to apply self-regulatory effort, an individual needs to be able to monitor any discrepancies between the current state and the standard as well as any progress that is taking place. Finally, one needs to be able to actually control behaviour in accordance with the desired direction (*Operate*). The result serves as input for the feedback loop. An individual becomes excited if the current state is in line with the desired state or standard.[14]

---

[13] Marleen Gillebaart (2018) Operational Definition of Self Control https://www.frontiersin.org/articles/10.3389/fpsyg.2018.01231/full, Retrived May 25th 2021

[14] https://www.frontiersin.org/articles/10.3389/fpsyg.2018.01231/full, Retrieved May 23rd, 2021

How to develop Self-Regulation and Control

1. ***Set a standard:*** You need a standard and goals for your desired end and aspiration. This should provide you with the big picture of what you want. Be very clear about what you want.

2. ***Develop Will Power and Confidence***: Develop a Can-Do Spirit and the confidence to say yes I can. To do this you need the willpower. Remember that you are in charge of your life and your life's outcomes depend mainly on the actions you take. So take charge of your life. Be in control of your decisions and take responsibility of the outcomes. The state of mind of being in charge has been proven to support will power and self-confidence. This self-motivation is needed to create the needed passion and enthusiasm to regulate your thoughts towards the desired end.

3. ***Prioritize:*** Prioritization has to do with planning and goal setting. You need to establish goals to accomplish your vision and purpose with milestones. Make sure important things and pre-requisites are placed above others. Goals often guide our choices. Ensure that the goals are specific so that you can achieve them and know that they have been achieved. This means the goals must be SMART (Specific, Measurable, Attainable, Realistic and Timebound). The more specific the goal, the better able people are to reach it. A highly abstract goal may not be actionable. For example, instead of pursuing the goal of "being healthy," a person may adopt the goal of "walking at least 30 minutes every day," which is more concrete and easier to monitor. Effective goal pursuits follow the SMART criteria.[15]

4. ***Remove temptation.*** People are not generally equipped to constantly resist temptation. It has been established that the way most people resist temptation is to remove the temptation in the first place or to move away from temptation. It is important to anticipate as much as possible the risk factor and put preventive mechanisms in place to avoid them, but should a risk or temptation

---

[15] Shahram Heshma, March 2017, Self-control strategies are key drivers of behavior change https://www.psychologytoday.com/us/blog/science-choice/201703/10-strategies-developing-self-control

arise, use your will power and thoughts of the consequences to mitigate it.

5. ***Monitor Yourself:*** Self-monitoring entails checking or measuring performance to see whether goals, values and principles are working, and if not, taking corrective actions. Monitoring provides feedback on performance. It is said that if something cannot be measured, it cannot be managed. Monitoring progress towards goal attainment helps one to concentrate on goal-relevant activities. For example, I noted that whenever I set a personal weight goal, and I checked my measurement, I was able to stay on course, but when there is no scale in my bathroom to weigh myself, I get off target. Lack of monitoring often undermines my weight management efforts. Self-monitoring helps us to stay committed to our goals and makes undesired habits much less difficult to change.

6. ***Manage Stress:*** Practising mindfulness and maintaining a healthy lifestyle is key to managing stress. When in the heat of the moment, stopping and taking a few deep breaths and counting up to seven silently are techniques that helps your heart rate slow down. Slowing down the heart allows you to relax in the moment. Exercising regularly, eating well, and getting enough sleep are healthy habits to help us to reduce stress. These healthy lifestyle practices help to improve focus, cognitive function and overall health. General mindfulness practices like meditation, Yoga, listening to cool music, quite me-time, and exercise, are all mindfulness practices that help to reduce stress. Exercise for example, allows better sleep, making you more refreshed and energized.

7. ***Develop Focus and Concentration.*** Focus is also key to success in every aspect of life. However, it may be difficult to focus without self-regulation. If you cannot regulate yourself well, many trivialities can turn you away from your purpose or delay and interrupt the achievement of the needed aims and goals. Self-regulation requires knowing and living your overarching purpose with focus. This means as much as possible, your personal plans and values will regulate you. Therefore, when you do not have clear personal plans and values, it would be difficult to focus and regulate yourself.

Try to focus on one goal at a time. Many people are easily distracted from core activities. To improve focus and concentration, it is important to manage distractions. Distractions can come from external sources or from internal sources, that is from within the individual. External sources of distraction may include social activities, friends, social media, text messages, phone calls, fun activities, sound or noise, light and many other stimuli. These may differ from person to person. Internal sources of destruction may include, stress, irritability, tiredness, low blood sugar level, exhaustion, anxiety, poor motivation, or internal disturbances.

Concentration can be improved by training the brain, playing some types of games that require concentration, like chess, crossword and jigsaw puzzles, scrabble, or monopoly among others. Listening to music has also proven to be very effective in improving sleep, thus concentration. Using a daily planner and sticking to it also helps to improve concentration. Meditation, spending time with nature, taking breaks and even moving to a new house all help in improving concentration and focus. Another important practice is pacing work into small bits so that work is done at a steady mindful pace rather than working with unstructured boosts of energy – also called the 20-mile rule.

Do you have a plan for yourself and are you able to stick to your personal and daily plans as much as possible? What are your personal values? Your values are the things that you believe are critical to the way you live and work. They (should) determine your priorities, and, often values are the measures you use to tell if your life is turning out the way you want it to[16]. What are your key personal do's and dont's?' List them.

For some people, personal values are what they desire. For example, desire in the arts to make people happy, perhaps learning to master the violin, or writing poetry, helping others, or working with children. For others, it may be attributes like service, care, loyalty, honesty, discipline, or excellence. If you do not have personal values, develop at least three, write them down, and post them where you can see them every day, just like your goals or milestones.

Self-regulation also refers to how we respond to challenges and new realities in our journey of life. Anyone can have dreams, but many people

---

[16] Mind Tools, https://www.mindtools.com/pages/article/newTED_85.htm, Retrieved 23RD May, 2021

cultivate wishful thinking which they call dreams. True dreams often come true for those who can persevere and pass the rough test of endurance. Life's actions are like a mixture of sand, pebbles and bigger stones. Often the stones are our top priorities, the pebbles are somewhat important and support the achievement of some big milestones, and the sand represents the many trivial things that demand attention from us. Many of us often focus on the many trivials, leaving the core of our lives, our top priorities behind. Prioritizing is our ability to put our stones ahead of our pebbles, and when we have enough time, attend to the many trivial things. Yet, many of us often put the sand and pebbles before the stones. This requires the mental and psychological strength to say no to disruptions, when the going gets tough, you need mental toughness to stay calm or firm in situations of uncertainty.

DEVELOPING EMOTIONAL INTELLIGENCE
FOR SELF-REGULATION AND CONTROL[17]

I found a quote by Oscar Wilde a blogger which I thought was interesting. It says, *"I don't want to be at the mercy of my emotions. I want to use them, to enjoy them, and to dominate them."*[18] This is why we need to develop and master emotional intelligence. Emotional intelligence, or EQ, is usually described as the ability to identify one's emotions and the control of those emotions while expressing oneself

I believe Emotional Intelligence is the skills for perceiving, analyzing and understanding our own and other people's emotions so that we manage them effectively to our advantage. Emotional Intelligence (EI) is measured by our Emotional Quotient (EQ). According to the APA dictionary of psychology, Emotional Intelligence is a type of intelligence that involves the ability to process emotional information and use it in reasoning and other cognitive activities[19]. Emotional Intelligence skills include:

- Self-awareness – of emotions and self-worth, and confidence in one's abilities. not to be taken advantage of.

---

[17]   https://positivepsychology.com/emotional-intelligence-skills/
[18]   Oscar Wilde
[19]   Dictionary.APA.org, 2018

- Empathy – high sense of understanding situations, diversity, compassion, and drive to assist others.
- Social Skills – skills in listening, conflict management, communication, and leadership.

Importance of Emotional Intelligence

In recent times emotional intelligence is considered critical for success in life. As a result several theories have been developed to explain the concept of IE each of which offer different perspectives on what EI involve. However, many of the theories have some commonalities. These convergence or commonalities include understanding personal emotions, the emotions of others, and managing both effectively. Though emotional intelligence has been proven to be neurologically linked to the brain, it has been established that EI skills are learnable.

Theories of Emotional Intelligence

Three emotional intelligence theories are presented here these include:

- The Four Branch Model of EI
- The Bar-On Model of Emotional-Social Intelligence (ESI)
- Goleman's Model of Emotional Intelligence

The Four branch model of Emotional Intelligence by Mayer and Salovey.

Mayer and Salovey proposed the Four Branch Model of Emotional Intelligence to explain the different skills required for Emotional Intelligence[20]. The Four Branch Model pushes forward that there are four distinct but inter-related Emotional Intelligence Skills. These are *Perceiving Emotions, Facilitating Thought Using Emotions, Understanding Emotions,* and *Managing Emotions.*

---

[20]   Mayer & Salovey, 1997; Salovey & Grewal, 2005

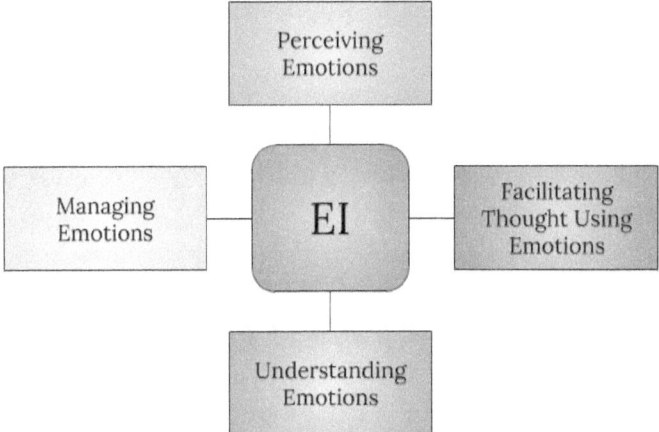

Source: Fiori & Vesely Maillefer, 2018[21]

Perceiving emotions has to do with reading our own emotions and other people's emotions. In order words awareness of your own emotions and being sensitive to other people's emotions by detecting and decoding emotional signals through body language, tone, and choice of words[22].

Facilitating thought using emotions has to do with how we analyse the emotions we perceive or detect and register the 'emotional information' for decision making on how to react or respond to the emotional information for decision-making, through rationalizing, problem-solving, and consideration of others' perspectives[23]

Understanding emotions refers the feedback we get from the analysis of the emotional information in order to manage the situation. This is how we understand the linkage different emotions, and how those emotions can be altered based on the situations we encounter, and how our understanding can alter our feelings over time[24].

Understanding emotions involves the ability to predict how someone's emotions are changing through their facial expressions, their tone of voice, and body language in general. Ability to predict or interpret emotional

---

21   Fiori & Vesely Maillefer, 2018 in Catherine More, 2018, Emotional Intelligence Skills, How to develop them. https://positivepsychology.com/emotional-intelligence-skills/ retrieved July, 2021
22   Papadogiannis et al., 2009
23   Mayer & Salovey, 1997; Mayer et al., 2002.
24   Mayer & Salovey, 1997; Mayer et al., 2002.

signals correctly determines the strength of our emotional management and communication skills.

Managing emotions deals with how we handle our own and other people's emotions effectively. Managing emotions relies on the earlier skills of perceiving or spotting emotions, facilitating thought, using emotions and understanding the emotions.

This means when you spot or perceive that someone is reacting negatively to your message, you have to quickly process that emotional thought, understand it and quickly alter your communication to alter the persons feelings. For example, while talking to someone on issues in a negotiation, I detected in the person's tone that all was not well. I could have also fired up and we both would have ended up in a loose-loose situation instead of a win-win situation. I quickly ended by changing my tone and facial expression and with a smile said, I am very committed to seeing this process through and will do my best to push through with it. You have my word. I immediately had a somewhat softer response. A colleague who was with me at the negotiation expected me to give it back to the man and make him know that the negotiation is not a master- servant relationship or a give and take relationship. At this point how do I use my knowledge of Emotional intelligence to manage the situation? Having perceived, spotted or picked the negative signal, I quickly remembered the facilitation thought process and the need to understand the situation by sometimes putting myself in the other person's shoes and imagine what could have made them react that way and try to respond rather than react. I quickly realized that our cultures and therefore the way we communicate some things are completely different. His understanding of how I had submitted my issues may have communicated something different from what I meant. Even if he understood what I meant but still reacted the way he did, I needed to focus more on the consequences of my respond and the outcome I expect at the end of the day to inform how I manage the emotions (both his and mine).

One key thing is that managing EMOTIONS is about managing ANGER. A Ghanaian proverb about emotional intelligence teaches "the mature/leaders do not squeeze their faces, the hold it tight at the exit". The book of proverbs of the Bible also adds "even fools are thought wise if they keep silent, and discerning if they hold their tongues[25]. Another quote from Budha says "Holding on to anger is like grasping a hot coal with the intent of throwing it at someone else: you are the one who gets burned[26]."

2. Goleman's Model of Emotional Intelligence

Daniel Goleman's work (1995) brought the need for emotional intelligence in leadership and management to the fore. Goleman presented 5 essential factors of emotional intelligence that determine an individual's EI or EQ.

1. *Emotional self-awareness* – which is very similar to Mayer and Salovey's *Perceiving Emotions* skill. This concerns awareness of one's own feelings, and encompasses an appreciation of how those feelings can affect those around us;
2. *Self-regulation*, which concerns managing one's own emotions and predicting their effects, in a similar way to *Facilitating Thought* and *Managing Emotions*.
3. *Motivation*, this covers continuing on when encountering obstacles;
4. *Empathy*, which relates to detecting others' emotions; and
5. *Social skills*, a set of Emotional Intelligence social skills that help us manage our interpersonal relationships and elicit certain reactions from them.

3. The Bar-On model of Emotional-Social intelligence (ESI)

Reuven Bar-On in 2006 proposed a more comprehensive model of Emotional and Social Intelligence (ESI) Model. Baron believes that emotional and social intelligence skills must go together because they can and do bear on our well-being and performance as humans[27]. Baron's Model therefore presents five interrelated competencies, skills, and behaviour clusters that were identified from existing scholarly literature. The 'clusters' are:

---

[25] The Bible, Proverbs 17:28, NIV
[26] Budha
[27] Bar-On 2013

1. Self-Awareness and Self-Expression; refers to your ability to express confidence not arrogance, ability to read and understand you own emotional sensations and how you express them. Can people easily read from your face or reactions what your feelings could be?

2. Social Awareness and Interpersonal Relationships. This refers to your ability to read peoples emotional reactions, nuances and how they affect your social relationships? Do you play well in a team? Are you sometimes blamed or confronted for hearsay or gossip? Do you know when to keep quiet and when to make your views and emotions known in a group?

3. Emotional Management and Regulation. This refers to how you keep your emotions under check when you become aware of them,

4. Change Management; deals with how you use feedback on your emotions and reactions to respond and make the needed improvements

5. Self-Motivation is the ability to keep on going when it appears difficult to do so.

The Bar-On model puts forward that the five clusters of emotional intelligence competencies and skills contribute to how people understand themselves and others, which informs how they express themselves, relate with one another and deal with everyday demands and believes that ESI is a good predictor of an individual's success in life. This assertion of Bar-On has been supported by neurological research in studies that show that brain damage to areas of various emotional functions and decision-making can impair our ability to function socially[28]:[29]. However, though EI is linked to the function of the brain neurologically, it can be learned through everyday experiences making it possible to develop our Emotional Intelligence skills.

---

[28] Bechra et al., 2000; Bar-On et al., 2003

[29] TalentSmart, 2018

Skills for Emotional Intelligence

Listening Skills.

Listening Skills is one of the most important EI skills. In EI, listening should not be limited to hearing or listening with the ears alone but listening with the eyes as well. This is because to perceive emotions and process it for effective understanding and management you need to analyse what you hear through the words, tone, paralinguistics, bodily symbols and general body language. It has been observed that only less than 10% of perceived communication comes from spoken words. The rest come from tone, voice, and bodily signs.

Omi works at a law firm, where brain storming sessions sometimes become quite frantic. Everyone tries to get their opinion heard, believing their idea is best. often, this leads to a lot of raised voices causing tension amongst the team. Josh dislikes it when others cut in when he is trying to get his point across, which he believes demonstrates very little respect and can lead to hurt feelings. Realizing Josh's body language Omi calmly suggests that people should listen quietly to one another when they are given the floor. By noticing Josh's withdrawal, when he said I have nothing more to say without completing his point, Omi perceived that Josh was not taking it very well emotionally. Omi used her intervention to try to manage emotions in the meeting. It's both recognition and effective handling of the team's emotions at play.

Others EI skills include:

Taking a deep breath when you notice negative emotional sensations, breathing deeply when anger attempts to take over; can be helpful

changing the discussion or subject matter

One effective way of managing emotions intelligently, is diverting or changing the topic in a subtle manner. This is akin to moving away from the temptation of anger or outburst.

Thinking before you speak

It is also important to read the room, the mode and the temperature before you speak so that you do not attract tension or outburst or negative response.

Distracting yourself; and writing about it.

Sometimes to keep yourself in check you need to turn your attention away by distracting yourself and keeping yourself busy, a Japanese may choose to do oregamy, you may choose to mind map or write or draw something or read your phone book.

SELF – REGULATION AND CONTROL AS CORE ASPECTS OF PERSONALITY QUOTIENT

Self-regulation and -control require intrapersonal and interpersonal skills. Intrapersonal skill entail knowing and understanding yourself, knowing your strengths and weaknesses, having self-confidence, being committed to your values, daring to be different, having the ability to execute personal plans and the ability to deal with adversity or challenges that come along, and respond rather than react to a crisis. This Intrapersonal intelligence is what I call the **Personality Quotient (PQ)** the main driver of personal leadership.

Personality Quotient (PQ) is a measure of the knowledge and understanding of one's self and individuality. I argue that the combination of a person's knowledge and understanding of self (PQ), one's reasoning abilities - Intelligence Quotient (IQ), ability to control and regulate one's emotion- Emotional Quotient (EQ), the knowledge and information you have (KQ), your ability to execute things you plan to do or have to do - Execution Quotient (XQ), The quality and worth of your relationships - Social Quotient (SQ) and your ability to solve problems and deal with challenges, crisis and uncertainties - Adversity Quotient (AQ) contributes largely to a person's success.

It has been put forward that one's Leadership Quotient is a measure of his/her intelligence quotient (IQ), Emotional Intelligence (EQ) and execution intelligence (XQ)[30]. However, I argue that Leadership Quotient must include one's Personality Quotient (PQ), (KQ), (SQ), and (AQ).

---

[30] Micheal Adwards, 2015, The Leadership Quotient: How IQ, EQ, and XQ Come Together for Great Leadership https://www.linkedin.com/pulse/leadership-quotient-how-iq-eq-xq-come-together-great-michael-edwards, Retrieved, November 17th 2021

This means that your Leadership Quotient, is a function (PQ), (IQ), (EQ), (KQ), (XQ), (SQ and (AQ). So I put forward that:

$$PQ + IQ + EQ + KQ + XQ + SQ + AQ = LQ$$

It is important to note that regardless of how high or low your IQ may be, what is important is to have a high PQ, EQ, KQ, XQ, SQ and AQ. Many people have great ambitions and dreams, which remain wishful thoughts because they never get past the thoughts stage. Many a time they may not know what to do or have the information that can bring about the needed change and impact they require. Other times too thoughts are not translated into actions. Execution ability is therefore an important measure of one's success. ***Thoughts without positive action is stupidity.*** In recent times, execution ability (XQ) is gaining strong prominence among many top companies and organizations in the world. If you can execute well but are not able to deal with challenges and adversity, you may not climb high. The ability to withstand adversity and persevere has been described by Paul G. Stoltz as the new science for success. This is what Stoltz calls the adversity quotient (AQ).

These seven soft skills (PQ, IQ, KQ, EQ, SQ, XQ and AQ) are what I call the twenty-first-century personal leadership skills. IQ and hard professional skills are required, but they should appear alongside the other twenty-first-century skills particularly PQ, KQ, XQ and AQ.

CHAPTER 5

PERSONAL LEADERSHIP PRINCOPLE 4

BE A MASTER OF YOUR LEADERSHIP QUOTIENTS:
(THE QUOTIENTS: IQ, KQ, EQ, SQ AQ, XQ, PQ, LQ)

INTRODUCTION

It is clear that the much-espoused stands about Intelligence Quotient (IQ) being a definitive trait for success has not stood the test of time. History has repeatedly demonstrated flaws in the notion that a high IQ can guarantee success in life. Other key quotients like Emotional Quotient (EQ), Social Quotient (SQ), eXecution Quotient (XQ), Adversity Quotient AQ have been shown to play a key role in achieving success in life. However, I like to add two others to the quotient theories. These are the Personality Quotient (PQ), and the Knowledge Quotient KQ.

Intelligence Quotient

IQ which stands for Intelligence Quotient is a measure of the intellectual abilities and potential of a person. IQ is designed to reflect a range of cognitive skills, such as reasoning, logic, and problem-solving. Normally an IQ score of 100 is considered average. An IQ of 1 to 24: is believed to signify profound mental disability, 25 to 39: severe mental disability, 40 to 54: moderate mental disability, 55 to 69: mild mental disability, 70 to

84: borderline mental disability, 85 to 114: average intelligence, 115 to 129: above average intelligence or bright, 130 to 144: moderately gifted, 145 to 159: highly gifted, 160 to 179: exceptionally gifted, while 180 and above is considered profoundly gifted[31].

We have heard statements like "he/she had learning and emotional disabilities and a low IQ of 78" and the conclusive assumption that the person may not be successful in life[32]. But history has repeatedly demonstrated major flaws in that school of thought. The highly successful and eminent can have IQs lower than average and people with very high IQs can be associated with relative obscurity. I decided to check for famous people who impacted our world but were considered to have low IQ. I was profoundly surprised at the list I found at one website. This list included Abraham Lincoln, the man who led and changed America so much, Mohammed Ali the legendry boxer who is quoted to have said, *I am the greatest not the smarteat"*, Dr. James Watson and his friend both Nobel Prize winners who discovered the DNA[33] among others. These people have proven that IQ is in fact not the key determinate of success. It is important to realize that IQ is a measure of intelligence which people are fundamentally born with but not a test of knowledge which is acquired through learning and experience. I believe that in the 21st Century, Knowledge and information is critically required for success, which is what I call Knowledge Quotient.

David Pulatie, senior vice president of Motorola Inc., notes that many people fall into hopelessness very early in life. This, I believe, is often the result of making wrong choices, or lacking the will and the strength to persevere against the odds. Unfortunately, life does not promise a bed of roses without thorns. Beautiful roses, just like life, have thorns, which ought to be dealt with if one is to behold the beauty that both offer.

Dr. Stoltz, author of *Adversity Quotient: Turning Obstacles into Opportunities*, notes that often what could have been, never gets a chance to

---

31

32 Kendra Cherry, August 2020, What is a Genius IQ? https://www.verywellmind.com/what-is-a-genius-iq-score-2795585, Retrieved 17th November 2021

33 Victoria Specter, 2017, Famous People with Low IQ, https://medium.com/@vicspec/famous-people-with-low-iq-690609a0500, Retrieved 17th December 2021

be because people either never tried or give up too soon on account of what he considers to be fear and doubt of their own capability. A friend once told me ***Fear is the worst enemy of progress and FEAR is False Evidence Appearing Real***. However, the disease of FEAR can be cured with faith. Faith according to Paul the Apostle "is the substance of things hoped for, the evidence of things not seen,"[34] in other words confidence. Hope is that which keeps a man going in the face of obstacles and challenging circumstances that appear so gloomy or unsurmountable. Faith is often expressed in the form of hope, courage, confidence and calm in the storms.

As I pondered over the subject of success in life, the following questions came to mind. Why do some people soar so high while others hover so low? What is the unique factor in each of our lives that will determine where we set our sights? And what forces will cause us to move closer to or further from realizing our cherished dreams and aspirations? What can we do to alter the outcome of our life, to make an extraordinary contribution over the course of our lifetime? I argue that there are some behaviours and characteristics that differentiate extraordinary people from those who settle for less, or those who do not participate at all to make a difference or take the right actions that would otherwise bring about a positive difference.

Leadership theories like the Great Man theory, trait theory, and skills theory put forward that to succeed, one needs intelligence and good relationship skills, which are determined by one's intelligence quotient (IQ), EQ and SQ, but I emphasize knowledge quotient (KQ), Personality Qoutient (PQ), eXecution Quotient (XQ),) and adversity Quotient (AQ).

For some time now, EQ has been regarded as the game-changer, the thing that makes the difference and separates successful people from those who do not succeed or get far in life. The emotional intelligence stance is in recognition of the limitations of IQ, the genetically influenced and scientifically measured aptitude that was long upheld by parents, teachers, and employers to be the definitive predictor of success. However, in recent years, it has been demonstrated over and again that both IQ and EQ alone are not enough. The case of Ted Kaczynski is one example of the limitations of IQ.

---

[34] Apostle Paul, Hebrews 11: 1, KJV Bible.

The Hermit of Harvard: A Case of the Limitations of IQ

It is abundantly evident that having a high IQ does not mean someone will be necessarily successful. There are many other factors about a person's personality and choices that determines personal success in life. There are numerous examples of people with high IQs who did not fulfil their potential in life. Many of us may have known brilliant people who have contributed far less than others who have moderate intellectual endowments. Ted Kaczynski was one of these low-performing brilliant people. Kaczynski was under investigation as the alleged Unabomber. He had all the indications of a high IQ. Stand-out smart since the time of his youth, he sprinted through high school, not bothering with his junior year. A wunderkind, he entered Harvard at the age of sixteen and graduated at twenty. He went on to complete his master's and PhD in maths at the University of Michigan, and then went on to teach at the world's premier maths department at the University of California at Berkeley. Teaching was the closest Kaczynski came to making a meaningful contribution to society. Yet, he quit his teaching job after two years.

Kaczynski was raised to develop his mind, but never developed his social skills or emotional intelligence. All the way through school, he was virtually invisible, socialising with no one and forming no enduring bonds. "Ted had a special talent for avoiding relationships by moving quickly past groups of people and slamming the door behind him," says Patrick McIntosh, one of Kaczynski's college roommates. Fellow townspeople in Montana described him as being socially removed. In college, he earned the nickname "the Hermit of Harvard."

Although Kaczynski demonstrated great ingenuity in allegedly creating and planting his bombs while evading the law, he was socially inept. Rather than contributing to the betterment of the world, he used his one strength, his intelligence, to kill three people and injure twenty-two.[35,36]

When I studied at the University of Ghana between 1997 and 2000, there were two popular professors, one with a double PhD, who had earned the highest accolades as class drunkards, and whom students publicly made fun of. IQ clearly falls short as a predictor of success. Kaczynski's case and the two drunkard professors are typical examples of how IQ is not a predictor of success. It also demonstrates that other aspects of life are equally important for a fulfilling and well-lived successful life.

Emotional Intelligence Quotient (EQ): The Perceived Panacea for Success

Recognizing the limitations of IQ as a predictor of personal success, Daniel Goleman insightfully explains why some people with high IQs flounder while many with modest IQs flourish. Goleman introduced a scientifically grounded and expanded notion of intelligence that redefined the word. In his best-selling book *Emotional Intelligence*, Goleman provides strong evidence for his concept and explained that in addition to an IQ, we each have an EQ, or emotional quotient. EQ is a measure of one's ability to self-regulate based on personal and social awareness and maturity.[37,38]

According to Goleman, EQ is the ability to empathize with others, postpone gratification, control your impulses, be self-aware, persist, and interact effectively with others. Citing several examples, Goleman argues

---

[35] Paul Stolz, 1997, Thriving in the Age of Adversity https://books.google. com.gh/books?id=xH5Jn9JYPF8C&pg=PA12&lpg=PA12&dq=Although+ Kaczynski+demonstrated+great+ingenuity+in+allegedly+creating+and+plant ing+his+bombs+while+evading+the+law,+he+was+socially+inept.+Rather+ than+contributing+to+the+betterment+of+the+world,+he+used+his+one+ strength%E2%80%94his+intelligence%E2%80%94to+kill+three+ people+and+injure+twenty-tw&source/ retrieved June 30, 2017

[36] Paul Stoltz,

[37] Beasley, K. (May 1987). The Emotional Quotient. Mensa Magazine (UK Edition), p25.

[38] Payne, W.L. (1983/1986). A study of emotion: developing emotional intelligence; self integration; relating to fear, pain and desire. Dissertation Abstracts International, 47, p. 203A (University microfilms No. AAC 8605928).

convincingly that, in life, EQ is more important than IQ. Just like IQ however, not everyone takes full advantage of their EQ, stopping short of their potential despite their valuable skills. However, because EQ lacks a valid measure and a definitive method of learning it, emotional intelligence remains elusive.

PQ

I believe that many people fall early into hopelessness and do not succeed because of low self-awareness, Low self-esteem, lack of confidence in one's own self, lack of understanding of one's self, one's uniqueness and one's individuality which I have described as personality quotient. (PQ). When people do not understand their individuality a uniqueness and their ability to surmount obstacles, they encounter on their journey of life they may fall short of their true worth and success. I have therefore added personality quotient to the literature and define it as the degree to which a person understands his/her individuality and uniqueness, a measure of self-confidence, purpose, passion, likes, dislikes, what works for you and what does not work for you, your strengths, weaknesses and your unique circumstances. Developing self-awareness is not easy because it develops and unfolds with time. To begin discovering yourself, you need to ask and answer the following questions:

- What am I living for?
- What are my Dreams and aspirations?
- What are my goals for the next 5 to 10 years?
- What are my strengths
- What are my weaknesses
- What makes me happy?
- What drives me?
- What are my triggers?
- What ae my Fears
- What are some of my key behavioural and thinking patterns (e.g what occupies my mind most of the time and what do I tend to use my time doing often) I link to

- What changes my thinking and behaviour (Religion, Culture, reading, videos, films?)
- What lowers my stress

eXECUTION QUOTIENT (XQ) – TURNING DREAMS INTO ACHIEVEMENTS

Do not Say I have a Dream, Say I have a Vision and a Plan of Action

How many times have you heard people say, I wanted to do something but..., or I thought of doing something but could not because of..., my plan was to, but I could not because ...." Whenever you hear such statements, then execution quotient (XQ), a measure of execution, ability is in question. The critical thing is not what you plan to do, but what you are doing to achieve your plan. XQ is a measure of one's ability to execute and perform effectively what you plan to do.[39] Many of us have beautiful plans that never happened. However, without a purpose, a vision and a goal, what do you execute?

Many of us do not have personal purpose and therefore do not have a vision or plans. We live by the day and allow each day to throw anything at us. We only have wishes and aspirations, dreams, but nothing more to make those aspirations and wishes manifest. If becoming a university professor is my vision, my goal would be to get a university degree, get a postgraduate degree, get a PhD, and get employment in a good university. Whatever I need to do to become a professor would be my goals and I need a plan to achieve those goals. I cannot become a professor by only wishing and sitting at home and praying to God to make me a professor. Doing nothing brings nothing, and doing less may bring less, and when that happens, we start to envy those who have made it.

When purpose, vision, goals and plans are not well-defined; and preparation is not adequate, we get poor performance and poor results.

---

[39] Koshima, H. (2001) Execution Quotient: "EQ". **Psychogeriatrics, 1,** pp. 153-154. Article retrieved from http://onlinelibrary.wiley.com/doi/10.1111/j.1479-8301.2001.tb00044.x/pdf. Retrieved March 2021

I know very intelligent people who do very little and blame their conditions on others or on their circumstances, refusing to realize that their situation could be self-imposed. Cast your mind back and think about some of the people you knew back then who were very intelligent, always among the top in class, but today are not as successful or impactful as some with average intelligence. To be effective and make a difference with your life, IQ, KQ and EQ, are definitely not enough, you need a high execution intelligence to follow through a well-defined personal purpose, vision, and goals with an actionable plan. Many people have perished with great ideas that never got executed because they feared, doubted themselves, or blamed one thing or the other.

Thomas Edison was told by his teachers he was 'he was too stupid it takes to learn in school'. He was fired from his first two jobs for being "non-productive."[40] However, he did not resign to fate or blame himself for being how he was described by his teachers, he went on to prove them wrong. He refused the label people wanted to tag on him. For Edison, scientific invention was not a mere wish or aspiration, it was a manifestation. Edison is reported to have invented the light bulb after about 1,000 unsuccessful attempts or failures. Though others believe that in reality, Edison was cunning enough to use the talents of other inventors (eg Nikola Tesla) to achieve his goal and that it was his business acumen that served him so well, which is easily relatable to the criteria listed below.

To invent, Edison had to put his IQ, EQ and XQ to work. But to succeed, he needed more than these three quotients, he needed skill (KQ) and a strong will to persevere (AQ). Without perseverance, Edison would not have achieved his goals.

Similar to, Edison, Albert Einstein, the all-time genius, as a child, was not recognised for his true potential; as often is the case, the education he received didn't cater for his unique talents, and as such he was regarded as no more than a capable student.[41]. Einstein, however, went on to win a Nobel Prize and altered the world's approach to physics. He had to rise above the descriptions or labels people gave to him. He had to demonstrate

---

[40]   MFP, But they did not give up, https://www.uky.edu/~eushe2/Pajares/OnFailingG.html, Retrieved June, 2021

[41]   https://www.uky.edu/~eushe2/Pajares/OnFailingG.html

his mental prowess through his scientific executions. He researched and acted on his thoughts and imagination to create the theory of relativity.[42]

In both the case of Edison and Einstein, their success was shaped by their thought, their actions, and their determination to persevere irrespective of how many times they failed. They were very focused and consistent. ***Thoughts without the requisite action is absurdity, action without thoughts is foolishness, but actions without perseverance may amount to nothingness.*** Perseverance is the net that sifts sand from the gravels and pebbles. It separates the ordinary achievers from successful and great people. It is measured by adversity quotient, and it is the new science of successful and great people. However, Einstein notes that "Insanity is doing the same thing over and over and expecting different results." We persevere not to get the same results but improved results.

ADVERSITY QUOTIENT—THE NEW SCIENCE OF SUCCESS

Contrary to Goleman, Paul Stoltz presents a compelling argument about what it takes to succeed and be great when he presented Adversity Quotient, which can be regarded as the new Science for successful and great achievers.

Adversity quotient is the ability to withstand a challenge or adversity and surmount it, or the ability to turn obstacles into opportunities. It requires purpose, passion, drive, focus, determination, patience, understanding, and perseverance. AQ forms the basis for critical thinking and problem-solving, which mere IQ or EQ may not offer. Stoltz argues that rather than IQ and EQ, important as they may be, it is adversity quotient (AQ) that makes the difference, because it combats self-defeating thought patterns. Stoltz adds, "IQ may have been a way to get the job, but AQ will keep you there."

While I was writing this section, I had an appointment with a woman who wished to discuss some banking products that her company was offering. I noted at the meeting that she was not herself. We started the meeting with a very informal discussion, and then she asked, "So how are you able to keep your balance?" I asked her with a smile, "Why do you

---

[42]   Ibid

ask?" Her reply was rather unexpected. "I don't understand why some bosses are so difficult to deal with; they won't appreciate anything you do, and they find the least opportunity to yell at you over the smallest mistake." She continued, "You know, I've observed how you relate to your team members. I noted that even when you're not satisfied with something, you stick to the issues; you don't attack the individual." She went on, saying, "Even while I waited to see you, I heard you ask one of them whether all was well, and you added, 'You don't appear well; are you sure everything is okay?' That's called emotional intelligence. That's exactly what a lot of bosses need."

My response was, "Yes, I agree, but if you have a boss with whom you're not comfortable, what do you do?" She replied, "You just find a better place." Then I asked, "What if the new place you find doesn't offer you the good climate you anticipate? Will you leave that place too, or resign yourself to fate?"

In my mind, I was wondering whether what this woman needed was AQ rather than EQ or both, so that she could stop shifting blame. It is often said, if you find you cannot change a thing or a situation change yourself. Some people possess a high IQ and all the aspects of EQ and XQ, yet fall tragically short of their potential. Stoltz concludes that neither IQ nor EQ appears to determine a person's success. Nonetheless, both play a role. The question remains, why some people persist, while others, perhaps equally brilliant and well-adjusted fall short, and still others quit?

According to Stoltz's AQ theory, there are three types of people: *quitters*, *campers*, and *climbers*.

Quitters are people who choose to drop out. Quitters abandon their pursuit to climb anytime they are faced with a challenge. Quitters, by definition, lead compromised lives. They refuse to take the opportunities presented to them. Quitters ignore, mask, or desert their core human drive to make a difference with their lives, and tend to blame someone or something for their situation. Quitters abandon their dreams and select what they perceive to be a flatter, easier path. The irony, of course, is that as life wears on, the quitter suffers far greater pain than that which they attempted to avoid by not climbing. Without a doubt, one of the most gut-wrenching, tormenting moments a person can face is when looking back on a life poorly lived. This is the quitter's fate. John Greenleaf put it this way: "For all the sad words of tongue and pen, the saddest are these: 'It might have been![43]'"

The second group of individuals is the campers. Campers go just a little farther, and then resign themselves to fate when difficulties set in, or they become contented with making a living rather than making a life. Campers simply say, "This is as far as I can [or want] to go." Campers prefer the plateau over the climb. They cease climbing and find a smooth, comfortable plateau where they can hide from adversity. There, they choose to sit out their remaining years. Campers, unlike quitters, at least take on the challenge of the climb, but they stop too early. Campers somehow diligently get as far as they go. The partial gain may be viewed by some as success. But this is a common misperception among people who view success as a specific destination, rather than a process. At any rate, although campers may have been successful in reaching the camp-ground, they cannot maintain their success without continuing to climb. It is lifelong growth and improvement process that defines the climb.

Stoltz refers to people who are dedicated to the lifelong ascent as climbers. Regardless of background, advantages or disadvantages, or misfortune or good fortune, they continue the ascent. Climbers are possibility thinkers and doers. They do not let anything stop them from continuing. They may fail, fall, or be stopped or chained, but situations are not limitations to them, remember the case of Nelson Mandela and his pursuit of leadership and fight against apartheid? Even when imprisoned, Mandela did not resign to fate, he planned, and worked, and went from prison to presidency as the first black President of South Africa. There may be constraints, but they're definitely not limitations. Not age, gender, race, physical or mental disability, nor any other obstacle can get in the way of the climber's ascent.

The current president of Gabon, Ali Bongo Ondimba, is a classic example of such a climber. Believed to have been raised in an orphanage and later adopted by Omar Bongo although denied[44], Ali ascended to the

---

[43] John Greenleaf, 5th March 2013, https://philosiblog.com/2013/03/05/for-all-sad-words-of-tongue-and-pen-the-saddest-are-these-it-might-have-been/, retrieved 13th May, 2021

[44] BBC News, 07th January 2019, Who is Who is Ali Bongo, president of Gabon? https://www.bbc.com/news/world-africa-46074728, Retrieved May 15th, 2021

presidency, irrespective of the controversies surrounding his birth and its constitutional implications, Ali did not settle to enjoy the largesse of his father Omar, the former President.[45] Dr. Kwame Nkrumah, Ghana's first president, and Jerry Rawlings, President and founder of Ghana's Fourth Republic, are other examples.

A Case of Adversity Quotient: When the Climb is Worth Dying For[46]

Mt. Everest is the highest mountain on earth and the place on earth that is closest to the stars. Many airliners often fly below its pinnacle. Daredevils often challenge themselves to make history by climbing to the top. Yet there are no guarantees that they will make it. Many perish and lose their lives in the process. Only one in seven who attempt the summit ever make it. Close to the pinnacle of the mountain, high-speed storms that blow through at one hundred miles per hour crush victims with triple-digit wind chills, fog, and zero visibility. Every climber dies a little, fighting a losing battle against cachexia, a syndrome of wasting away marked by loss of weight, muscle atrophy, fatigue, and weakness. Above eighteen thousand feet, cuts don't heal easily, the body is depleted, and the air is so dry that a cough literally fractures the ribs. To climb amid such adverse conditions is the ultimate test of human endurance.

On Friday, May 10, 1996, thirty-one climbers from five expeditions reached the summit of Mt. Everest. Suddenly, a fierce storm swept through, causing many of the climbers to be stranded. A few hours' later, some had died, while others remained alive.

One climber's experience, Beck Weathers, teaches us about luck and tenacity and questions when the climb is worth dying for, when to take on a climb and when not to, when to go on and when to stop? Weathers lay unconscious in the snow when the storm broke. During the night, a rescue team found Weathers, but thought it was impossible to save him. It was too dark, the trail was too treacherous, and Weathers was too far gone.

---

[45]   This is Africa, 2014, Biafra's Forgptton Children, https://thisisafrica.me/politics-and-society/biafras-forgotten-children/, Retrieved 2nd May, 2021

[46]   This case is largely adapted from Paul Stoltz, *The Adversity Quotient: Turning Obstacles into Opportunities,1997.*

However, a few hours later, Weathers stirred. Something deep within saved him from his icy doom and awakened him to his grim situation.

According to *Newsweek*, Weathers reported, "I was on my back on the ice. It was colder than anything you can believe. My right glove was gone, my hand looked like it was moulded of plastic." "Weathers had every reason to give up. He had taken on the mountain and lost. He lacked supplies, his team, shelter, and any probability of survival. While confronted with his end, Weathers somehow triggered the inner resolve to take on a mountain bigger than he had ever climbed before, the mountain of survival against hope. Frozen, exhausted, alone, and barely alive, Weathers had to somehow move, stand, and navigate the treacherous journey back to base camp".[47]

A deep sense of purpose and connection to others spurred him to action. Lying there in the snow, he said, "I could see the faces of my wife and children pretty clearly. I figured I had three or four hours to live, so I started walking." To Weathers, the next few hours seemed like centuries. Knowing that to rest meant certain death, he somehow kept moving. Weathers stumbled upon what looked like a blue rock. Fortunately, it was a tent. His team hauled him inside; his clothes were so stiff with ice that they had to cut them away. They put a hot water bottle to his chest and gave him oxygen. No one expected Weathers to survive. Due to the unexpected adversity brought on by the storm, others with greater skill, even world-famous mountaineering guides such as Scott Fischer, died. In fact, Weathers' wife had already received a message that her husband had died, only to find out hours later that he had somehow lived. No one had accounted for that element inside Beck Weathers that enabled him to survive against such insurmountable odds while so many others perished. Weathers lost his right arm below the elbow and all five fingers on his left hand, as well as parts of both feet, and his nose, which was later reconstructed. Would you have survived? Some may attribute Weather's survival to luck, and some may call the urge to go for such a challenge foolhardiness.

Life is like mountain climbing. Fulfilment is achieved by relentless dedication to the climb, sometimes slowly, by slow painful steps. Scaling the mountain is an indescribable experience, each one with his own

---

[47]   Stolz, Paul, Praise for Adversity, Turning Obstacles into opportunities, Pg.52, The case was largely adopted from the sources.

approach and speed, one that only climbers can understand and share. With the exhaustion comes success, a sense of achievement, satisfaction, and a sense of joy and peace as refined as the mountain air. It is, however, important to know what mountains to take on in life, and for what purpose. If it is not to make your life and other people's life better, would it be worth the climb if the price is too dear?

In 2007, I climbed Mount Fløya, in Tromso, which rises 671 meters above the ocean. Mount Fløya is a popular location for both a great adventure and a panoramic view of Norway's Arctic city. I was determined to finish the climb. Before I set off, I felt unwell, and there were several comments made that should have discouraged me, but I was so determined. I planned and prayed for the climb because that was to be my first experience at climbing a mountain of that magnitude. The day came, and those of us who had registered were taken to the base. The experience is not something to describe, it must be experienced. Many dropped out along the line. When the going got so tough, I almost turned back. But I realized I had gone too far to turn back, yet moving forward seemed impossible. As I lay on the mountain cliff, scared to look down or back, gasping for air, I could only muster what felt like it were to be my last prayer. Then suddenly, I remembered Victor Frankl, "After all, man is that being who invented the gas chambers of Auschwitz; however, he is also that being who entered those gas chambers upright, with the Lord's Prayer or the Shema Yisrael on his lips." The thought of that prayer and the power within me to survive against the odds spurred me on.

Victor Frankl put it this way: "That which must give light must endure burning." It is important to be rational and realistic about the climb and strike a fine balance between bravery or courage and foolhardiness. As I was pondering over these thoughts while lying on the floor, there came an angel, Bata Kone. Bata had indicated in an earlier conversation that he had climbed mount Catherine at the peak of the Sinai Peninsula in Egypt. Bata encouraged me, gave me a little water, and helped me move on. This energy I felt will be stored and passed on to another who was struggling on their climb. We need others to help us navigate the climb. Those who stay encamped may be justified, as they have less risk because they feel warmer and safer, but they will never feel the rarefied joy and pride that comes with completing the climb.

Success comes in different grades and sizes and can be defined as the degree to which one moves forward and upward, progressing in one's lifelong mission despite the obstacles and other forms of adversity. So, success is relative to purpose and goals. Our personal mission defines our life's journey and success. Learning from Beck Weathers, you need to be prudent about which mountain you chose to climb on your life's journey. The climb should indeed be worth dying for. Like Weathers, I do not know how much time you have left, but you may as well start moving now.

A DIFFERENT PERSPECTIVE OF SUCCESS: NAK'S STORY48 - DON'T LET YOUR CIRCUMSTANCE DEFINE YOU

Distinguished Professor Emeritus of Psychology and Management Mihaly Csikszentmihalyi, Founder, Co-Director, Quality of Life Research Centre, also of the University of Chicago defines success as something that helps others and at the same time makes you feel happy as you are working at it. This definition was derived from his work on what he calls "FLOW, the secret of happiness", which he discovered from interviews with very respected successful CEOs[49]. From this definition, success is not merely an end goal to attain but a journey in which success is experienced through satisfaction as the process unfolds. NAK's Case, perhaps typifies this definition of success.

NAK's Case

Years ago, Professor Mihaly Csikszentmihalyi of the University of Chicago, from whose work this case is adapted, reported that he had

---

[48] The first half of this section is adapted from Mihaly Csikszentmihalyi of the University of Chicago. The first name of the subject, Nak, is an artificial one, composed of letters from names used in many languages. This is to depict the cross-cultural applicability of the story. The case is adapted from the Thierry Graduate School of Leadership, Belgium.

[49] Mihaly Csikszentmihalyi 2004, FLOW, the Secret of Happiness, TED Talk, https://www.cgu.edu/people/mihaly-csikszentmihalyi/ https://www.ted.com/talks/mihaly_csikszentmihalyi_on_flow?language=en, retrieved 6th June, 2021

studied at a place where railroad cars were being cleaned up and repaired. The main workplaces were huge and unclean hangars, with constant noise that made it difficult for people to hear. Many of the lower-level workers who worked there hated their jobs and were constantly watching the clock in anticipation of closing time. As soon as they were out of the factory, some rushed to a pub, and others drove home fast in the hope of finding their better life there. But one of them stayed.

The one who stayed was Nak, a barely literate man in his early sixties who had trained himself to understand and to fix every piece of equipment, from the cranes to the computer monitors. He loved to take on machinery that didn't work, figure out what was wrong with it, and set it right again. At home, he and his wife built a large rock garden on two empty lots next to their house, and in that garden, Nak built misty fountains that made rainbows, even at night, through reflective mechanisms. The hundred or so people who worked in the same hangars respected Nak, even though they didn't fully understand him. They asked for his help whenever there was any problem. Many claimed that without Nak, the hangars might as well close.

Nak's story could have happened in many places in the world because many of us find ourselves in situations of helplessness or hopelessness. Often, many of us also do not have a clear definition of our purpose and mission in life, and how we can achieve our purpose and navigate the challenges we face. Our ability to understand who we are, our strengths and weaknesses, rising above limiting conditions like level of education, living with job conditions that we do not desire, expecting so much from our job without considering how we ourselves contribute to our welfare at work and in life, living for a purpose that we are not suited for and recognizing that no one else but us has the key to our happiness, are key considerations for personal success. What do you think made Nak so different? Was it his IQ or EQ, or something else not defined by both IQ and EQ? Why is there beauty and harmony in Naks work, but not in his work environment? Is it education, training, or learning in general that makes the difference for a positive life? Or is having a positive life primarily about attitude toward life and behaviour? Where do personal motives and drives fit in the picture in Naks case? What I learn from Naks case is that there are conditions that we cannot control, neither can others control.

For example, we cannot control who our parents are or where we were born, but there are also situations that we can and do control, for example, choosing our friends and what we do with our time. We also choose to be happy or sad, irrespective of the circumstances. Our choices, actions, and our decision to be happy and create the world we want around us is entirely our decision.

KNOWLEDGE QUOTIENT (KQ)

I have not come across Knowledge Quotient in any literature yet. It is therefore my new introduction into the literature. As mentioned earlier, I consider KQ to be a measure of the knowledge and information that a person possesses or that is available to a person at any given time. Though I have not developed a system of measurement for KQ, I believe that in the information and digital age, knowledge, skill and information are critical to success.

Many people have great dreams and aspirations, but they do not know what to do. Some know what to do but they do not have the knowledge and skills to accomplish it, so then they are not successful. The more you have relevant knowledge, skill and timely information that you can use, the more likely you are to succeed. In an article in the Nigerian Gaurdian, Lanre Olusola a contributor noted

"knowledge is Power," This statement is as accurate as you can ever imagine. Few people understand how important knowledge can be. Knowledge is what prevents us from making the same mistakes we made in the past. Without knowledge, one cannot be successful in life. Knowledge is key when it comes to shaping our personality, behaviour and dealings with people. Successful men and women have put their knowledge to good use and have reached noble heights, being remembered for long on this earth. Knowing the importance of knowledge, people must look to the potential avenues to gain knowledge and make use of it positively"[50.]

---

[50] Lanre Olusola, September 2018, the power of knowledge and Success in Life, https://guardian.ng/features/the-power-of-knowledge-and-successful-life/, Retrieved 17th November, 2021

Lanre's view supports my point on the importance of KQ and I wondered why we have not considered that in the quotients theory yet, so now I introduce you to KQ. Build your KQ and it will serve you well. Seek to know and to learn. Be a lifelong learner. The internet abounds with various learning sites, videos and books. There are also a myriad of news sites for information by the click of a button. There are also skills development sites and networks. Develop a list of sites where you can continuously learn. In a world of constant change, you get outdated and obsolete if you are learned. You must be a learner, a lifelong learner. Eric Hofer said, "In times of change, learners inherit the earth, while the learned find themselves beautifully equipped to deal with a world that no longer exists." It is advised in all your getting get knowledge and wisdom and when you have it get understanding[51]. However, no matter how knowledgeable you are if you cannot put your knowledge to use, it is useless.

PERSONAL DEVELOPMENT (KQ) AND SUCCESS

Self-development entails how we plan to change and improve our lives. Many of us have strengths in the form of talents, but not abilities. Often we feel too contented with the status quo. One way of developing ourselves is by developing skills and abilities through education, training, and lifelong learning. Education is not mere schooling, but a lifelong affair. Whoever does not develop through lifelong learning will find himself equipped to deal with a world that no longer exists when change arrives. Great leaders are great learners. We need knowledge, skills and attitudes to make our lives meaningful and fulfilled, not mere qualifications. These days, many people have qualifications but lack the skills and attitudes to back up those qualifications.

Though qualified, some people cannot play in teams, for example; they easily get offended and take offence so much that their abilities become boxed within them. Some lack self-respect and control. Others lack the urgency and discipline to get things done, and still others lack initiative and the personal drive. Some cannot take responsibility for

---

51   Provers 4:7 of the Bible.

anything that goes wrong; they have to look for something to blame. Some people lack accountability; others are impatient and lack respect for authority and structure. These things are not qualifications; they are soft skills and attitudes that are required to propel hard qualifications to the needed heights. Without skills and attitudes, qualifications are nothing, because they cannot assert much.

So personal development goes way beyond getting another qualification. It is about developing a set of skills and attitudes that will create the environment for you to make a meaningful contribution with your life. The poet W. H. Auden wrote the following:

> If we really want to live, we'd better start at once to try;
> if we don't, it doesn't matter, but we'd better start to die.

The choice seems simple: in the time span between today and the unavoidable end of our days, we can choose either to live, or to exist, or even die. Biologically, life is organic and an automatic process as long as we take care of the body. But to live in the sense of making a life and in the sense that the poet meant is by no means something that will happen by itself. Making a life is not an automatic process. In fact, everything seems to work against it. If we don't take charge of life's direction, then our life will be controlled by the outside, to serve the purpose or meaning of some other party. Both inner and outer factors influence our lives; however, as we cannot reasonably expect anyone to make us live, though they may help us, we should perhaps discover how to do it by ourselves, regardless of where we fit in any given environment.

CHAPTER 6

PERSONAL LEADERSHIP PRINCIPAL 5: THE WAY AND THE POWER TO SEE THE RIGHT WAY

The way, and the power to see the right way. - Joshua Bortey Alabi Jnr[52].

I asked an unsuspecting twelve-year-old what he thinks makes people successful in life. His answer made my jaw drop in awe. He said: "The way, and the power to see the right way". I took a deep breath and asked again, he repeated, and then I asked him to tell me what he meant. He said "many times you are confused, and you do not know what to do. Sometimes you are afraid to ask your parents or your teachers, so you ask your friends, but they can also give you bad advice, and then you will not be successful. But when you know the way, and you have the power to see the right way, I think you will be successful." I then asked him, "so why did you say power to see the right way." He said "sometimes you think your friends' advice is wrong, but you find it difficult to say no to them. If you have the power to say no to bad advice, and if you can say no to yourself when you think something is bad, I think you can be successful." The views expressed by the twelve-year old boy informed the content in this chapter. It took me several days to ponder over his wise words – "The Way and the Power to See the Right Way."

---

52   A quote from Joshua Bortey Alabi when he was twelve years old and asked what he believes makes a man successful?. The quote inspired the chapter.

I then came to a simple conclusion about the difference between the way, and the power to see the right way by pondering over my own life experiences and the many stories I have heard in class or read about. The simple conclusion is that choices, and the ability to make the right choices in life, can make you successful. That is what this chapter is all about.

Ultimately, our choices influence our success in life to a very large extent. The profession or career you choose, the wife or husband you choose, the friends you choose, where you choose to live, what you choose to value, how you choose to look at life, these can go a long way to determine whether you succeed or fail. I can go on and on about our choices. Our success depends on our choices – period. Your choice is the "Way" and the ability to make the right choices and stick to them is the "Power to see the Right Way."

Life is full of choices and dilemmas. Your life's output and outcomes are a product of the choices you make, the people we choose to have around us, and our actions and inaction. These choices are loaded with decisions about the way to go and finding the right way. My understanding is that "the way and the power to see the right way" can be seen in two ways. Firstly, the way relates to our core choices and decisions in life, which informs other peripheral choices. The power to see the right way entails the ability to judge the worth and consequences of those choices before taking them, even though it does not always end up being the same way we may expect. The "way" we choose should be informed by our core purpose or meaning in life and our values. Unfortunately, many people do not know their purpose in life, therefore their choices are not guided, and as such, any wind can blow them in any direction.

However, sometimes choices are made for us earlier on in life when we did not have any control over our choices. For example, we do not and cannot choose our parents, birthplace or in many cases, the first schools we attend. Other times our choices are influenced by society and other people's expectations. That is why we find that some children end up very far from their true calling in life. This is because at the time they had no or little control over their career or profession, their parents forced them to attend schools and training programmes in school that were not in line with their purpose and passion. So we need to identify our purpose in life so we can make guided choices early enough. We need to understand who we are, our personality and our personal capital, to understand our calling and mission in life. This is treated in detail under the four capitals.

On the other hand, the power to see the right way relates to our ability to see the right courses of action to pursue our core purpose in life. Have you found your purpose in life yet? What courses of action are the right way for you to accomplish your purpose? Write them down.

The second view of the "way and the power to see the right way" is that even when the right choices and actions are discovered and taken, what matters is not our action, but our intentions and the methods we use. In addition, the behaviours associated with the choices and actions we take, could make a right action valid or not. For example, you decide to go to school and become a Medical or Juris Doctor, but when you got to medical school or law school, you did not study. Yes, you saw the way, but your behaviour did not have the power of the right way. Another example is a professional who decides to go for a networking dinner to improve his network, but got there and over-indulged in alcohol, or someone who decides to work on stocks, but chooses to add gambling. The process of self-discovery is a journey. Do not worry, when you realise some mistakes you may have made in the past or find yourself changing your mind about what you thought you ought to be doing.

This second aspect is what defines the power to see the right way. Arguably, what may be right in one context may not be right in another context. However, from a moral standpoint, some behaviours may never pass the test of prudence or acceptability irrespective of the context. So the question is - How can we guide our actions and insulate ourselves from the pressures of the wrong way? Personally, as I pondered this question, I made a list of the pressures that can lead to the wrong way, and these included:

- the pressure of fear
- pressure to please others against your wishes
- pressures of ego that come in the form of arrogance or
- pressure from the urge to maintain some standards of life, or
- pressure from envy, the desire to be like someone else, or to undermine others we consider to have something we do not have

These were a few of the pressures that could hinder us from seeing the right way. I am not suggesting that we should not strive to improve our quality of life or our standards of living. Nonetheless, how we should achieve what we desire lies in the power to see the right way – not from undue pressure. This is why many people may have many academic qualifications, or fantastic amounts of money, but because they do not have the power to see the right way, they sometimes end up in trouble, or even waste their lives and acquisitions. ***Rather than focusing on the Pressure, focus on the Purpose, so you can see the right way more clearly.*** Let's look at two examples where pressure rather than purpose blurred the right way leading to failures. I present the cases of the lighthouse keeper, and Krupp's story, to demonstrate the way and the power to see the right way.

A lighthouse keeper is responsible for tending and caring for a lighthouse, particularly the light and lens in the days when oil lamps and clockwork mechanisms were used. Keepers were needed to trim the wicks, replenish fuel, wind clockworks, and perform maintenance tasks such as cleaning lenses and windows. The duty of the Light housekeeper is to safely guide ships through treacherous waters, which is incredibly significant to a nation's maritime sector and its safety. The main resources needed in a lighthouse were the fuel, the lantern and the lighter. All of these must be available at any given time.

Now consider the story of the lighthouse keeper and Krupp's story.

The Lighthouse Keeper[53]

A lighthouse keeper worked on a rocky stretch of coastline and received his new supply of oil once a month to keep the light burning. Not being far from the shore, he had frequent guests.

One night, a woman from the village begged for some oil to keep her family warm, and the lighthouse keeper gave her some. Another man asked for some for his lamp. Another requested the kind lighthouse keeper to give some of the oil to lubricate a wheel. Since all the requests appeared reasonable, the lighthouse keeper tried to please everyone by granting all the requests. Close to the end of the month he realised the supply of oil

---

[53] The Story of the Light House Keeper is adapted from John Maxwell's "Developing the Leader Within You

was very low. Soon it was gone, and the beacon went out. That night, several ships were wrecked, and lives were lost. When the authorities probed, the man was very remorseful. He pleaded, but the authorities responded, "You were given oil for one purpose - to keep the light burning! Ships were wrecked and several lives were lost because you sacrificed the purpose to the pressure of requests." The light housekeeper failed because he sacrificed his purpose to the pressures of request and lack of power to say no to others. He satisfied other people's requests at the expense of his purpose. What are the pressures and requests in your life right now? The way is often defined by purpose and the power to see the right way is often derived from purpose and the ability to see clearly under pressure. There is a Ghanaian Ga proverb that says "do not remove the thongs while in the thongs". This means, when under pressure or in crisis, do not fret or be in a hurry to make decisions, keep calm and think the situation through well before you make a decision. The lighthouse keeper did not see the right way himself because he lost sight of his purpose, either because he did not take time to think about the consequences, or he did but did not have the power to say no when under pressure of requests. Purpose would have directed him and shown him the way, but the power to see the right way has to do with one's willpower and self-discipline to choose the way purpose prescribes. When we allow purpose to guide us, we can often see the right way, but the ability to take the right way, the moral high ground, has to do with our will power. However, when we are motivated by selfishness, greed or ego, or the desire to be accepted by all or to please all, we may often miss the right way. *Life is full of dilemmas, but the ability to choose the right way in times when we are at the crossroads is to stay connected to our purpose and values - our mission in life.* The lighthouse keeper missed the right way because he did not have the will-power to resist the woman who begged for oil to keep her household warm and the subsequent request. *Do not allow pressures from others to lead you onto the wrong path.*

Krupp's Story[54]

"Alfried Krupp was an entrepreneur who built a steel company in the middle of the nineteenth century. Krupp was so obsessed with the loyalty of his employees that he chose paternalism as a means to maintain loyalty. Krupp believed that by attending to the welfare of his employees, he could make them loyal to the organization and make them more productive. As a leader, he provided his workers with housing, schooling, health care, training, small loans at low interest, and so on, creating a budding welfare state. The workers expressed their appreciation by proudly calling themselves "Kruppianers" and gave their loyalty to the company and the Krupp family for an entire century. But the Krupp's example also shows the need to think about the consequences of our decisions and choices on ourselves, others and future generations.

Krupp's protectiveness was a key factor, and perhaps the cause of the final collapse of the Krupp family investment. Though the over-expansion after World War II could be a key factor to the collapse, it is believed that the expansion was largely motivated by the need to live up to the Krupp promise that every Kruppianer would forever have a job. It could also be considered an ego driven urge to be the largest steel company in the world. This ultimately brought the company to the verge of collapse. The family was expelled from management by the German government and the banks in order to save the business. Lots of loyal Kruppianers had to be laid off when they most needed the jobs – in the midst of a serious recession in the German coal and steel industry when jobs were harder to find. Krupp also, like the light housekeeper, lost sight of his purpose and the purpose of the organization, resulting in many wrong choices which accounted for the demise of the company.

These two stories reflect the reason why the meaning, purpose and mission, of other persons or organizations have to be parallel with that of individuals. Krupp's approach of an "assured bottle-feed" created a growing state of dependency which deprived many people of their real meanings in life. Krupp's account was also motivated by ego and an unrealistic goal.

---

[54] *Gilman, D. C.*; Peck, H. T.; Colby, F. M., eds. (1905). *"Krupp Foundries, Social Work at"*. *New International Encyclopedia*(1st ed.). New York: Dodd, Mead.

Where does living for others, making a difference in people's lives, and knowing the responsibility that we bear towards other people who depend on us, or to an unfinished task connect? Where should we draw the line and balance between the unfinished tasked and the person who affectionately waits for us? Viktor Frankl, the author of the seminal book Man's Search for Meaning in Life, said "A man who knows the responsibility that he bears towards another man who affectionately waits for him or to an unfinished work, shall not throw away his life, he knows the why of his existence and shall bear with almost anything." Was he suggesting that we take on other people's irresponsibility's as our responsibilities by robbing them of their true meaning in life? Could that also be perpetuating the self-pity of the people whose responsibilities we unduly take on ourselves? To what extent does taking on other people's responsibility make us know the why of our existence? This is explained under the fourth capital, the spiritual capital, in part two of this book.

When does empathizing rob people of their true meanings in life? Focus on the purpose and do not be swayed by other people's minor interests or other pressures of life.

IDENTIFYING THE WAY

Identifying the way for life's journey should begin with an understanding of one's purpose and calling in life, one's values and principles and what makes one different from others with a similar calling. Unfortunately, many of us are not aware of our mission in life. We are sometimes not conscious of our values. Our ability to identify and understand these factors have to do with our personalities, our experiences, our expectations, and the culture and value system of the environment we find ourselves in. Many of the decisions and choices we make as people are often informed by our interest, values or the things we have heard, seen, or experienced. Consequently, these forces influence our ability to see the way.

But the question is how we find a way when there is no destination in mind. To define the way, we must first know where we are going. We must have a clear VISION. The destination defined by our vision presents us with a myriad of options about which way or path we may take. Often, there are many routes to our destination, but the challenge is how to see the right way. Our choices sometimes do not end up being exactly where we expect them to be. Sometimes good luck counts, but not without the bad because the bad often leads to learning and new opportunities. For example, we discover that our child likes to dress her dolls or cares about people, so we want them to become a fashion designer or a medical officer. We plan their education, get them to go to school and study science, but they fail along the way. However, college education may not be the only route. The fact that one path failed does not mean they cannot get to their destination. Once we focus on the purpose, we can get to the destination, though the goals and the route may change. However, knowing when to change courses of action or the way is also a key part of knowing the right way. Our goal is often to navigate life's contours smoothly and avoid unpleasant consequences. In other words, minimize the effects of bad luck. So how can we do this? Christine Walker, author of the book A Painter's Garden: Cultivating the Creative Life, states "it is not enough to dream, although it is necessary to have a clear vision. Parents and teachers praise hard work, but many of the wise advocate effortlessness. Faith ranks high, but one's faith is always tested. Good luck counts but not without the bad, because that often heralds good fortunes. Talent, knowledge and skill in one's chosen field are required, but naivety and openness to learning sometimes brings profound insights and a wealth of good ideas. Regardless of the path we take, getting "there" never ends up being exactly where we think it is going to be."[55]

"One is always learning from nature, the great teacher, who says it is ok to be out of control, a little confused, a tireless worker and a reflective spirit. On life's journey, one may make mistakes and not be too oriented towards results. We may have ideas about how we want our garden to be, but it tells us quite clearly how it wants to grow."

There are many things in life that nature puts out of our control without explanations. There are many times that we find ourselves at the cross-road. When at the cross-roads, our ability to see the way depends on the extent to which we allow our purpose, values and principles to guide us. However, there are situations in which relying on ourselves is not enough.

[55]   Christine Walker, 1997 "A Painter's Garden: Cultivating the Creative Life", Warmer Books Inc. New York, pp.2-3, ISBN 0-46691208-5

There are times that we need a cause greater than ourselves as a sanctuary to rely on. When our fears, outrun our hopes, we need a source to draw inspirations from. Who or what do you rely on in times of dilemma or difficulty? Some call it the transcendent, others call it God, whatever you may wish to call it, you need a sanctuary to fall on in time of a need for clarity about the way. Even with the vision, purpose and values, one needs prayer and meditation for God's direction and confirmation. Do not rely on your own understanding but lean on God for all your directions and he will make your paths clear[56].

However, when your vision is blurred and the destination is itself not clear, how do you find the way? It is important to develop our personal vision statements and know our values, though we may sometimes be misled and get off-track about this. Many of us do not recognize that we always need others to help us refine our ideas and identify our own blind spots, which I call the "Critical Support Group", a group of people known to you who make up for you where you are short, particularly for thinking through various aspects of your life's journey. It could be career, family, investments, academics, business etc. Blind spots can often hinder our ability to see right. However, any advice you receive must go through your own process of sifting to make sure that in the end, it is your decision, your choice, and not that of the person advising you. Sometimes bouncing our ideas or issues by people is a good way of clarifying the path. But going to God in prayer or meditation, helps to direct our path.

The power to see the right way depends on our ability to learn, irrespective of where the learning comes from. It requires knowing when to change our cause of action, or when to keep going, or when to go left or right because of new knowledge, information or learning, and when to stick to our original cause of action. This is what I call ambidexterity of life.

EGO AND THE POWER TO SEE THE RIGHT WAY

Ego deprives a lot of us from seeing the right way. When we put our faith in objects which we hold as symbolisms or status symbols of what we represent, or who we are, our ego clouds our ability to see, and that

---

[56]   The Bible, Proverbs chapter 3:-6, NKJV.

often becomes counterproductive. For example, some of us are defined by our titles, positions, qualifications, affiliations, possessions and wealth. This ego driven sense of identify blinds us from seeing reality. Eckhart Tolle, a bestselling author featured on Oprah's Super Soul Sunday, puts it this way in his book Awakening to Your Purpose: "To recognize one's own insanity is of course, the arising of sanity, the beginning of healing and transcendence."[57] We cannot heal our vision if we do not first heal our thoughts and perceptions. Tolle defines ego as "any image you have of yourself that gives you a sense of identity—and that identity derives from the things you tell yourself and the things other people have been saying about you that you've decided to accept as truth", but I add, irrespective of reality.

EGO-KILLS: A STORY OF HUMAN NATURE

Peer Mohamed Sardhar started a discussion on the web and told this interesting story about the dangers of ego. There was once a learned scientist. After a lot of practice and effort, he developed a formula and learned the art of reproducing himself. He did it so perfectly that it was impossible to tell the reproduction from the original.

One day, while doing his research, he realized that the Angel of Death was searching for him. In order to remain immortal, he reproduced a dozen copies of himself. The reproduction was so meticulous that all of them looked just like him. Now, when this Angel of Death came down, he was at a lost to know which of the thirteen before him was the original scientist, and confused, he left them all alone and returned to heaven.

But, not for long, for being an expert in human nature, the Angel came up with a clever idea. He said to the scientist, addressing all thirteen of them, "Sir, you must be a genius to have succeeded in making such a perfect reproduction formula. However, I have discovered a flaw in your work, just one tiny little flaw."

The scientist immediately jumped out and shouted, "Impossible! Where is the flaw?" "Right here" said the Angel, as he picked up the scientist from among the reproductions and carried him off. The whole

---

[57]   Eckhart Tolle (2006,) New Earth: Awakening to Your Life's Purpose, pg14

purpose of the scientist and his formula of reproduction failed as he could not control his pride and lost his life. So while one's Knowledge and Skills can take one to the top of the ladder and make one successful, the three-letter word "EGO" can pull one down easily.

The Dual Perspective of life and
The power to see the way

One of the principal gods of Roman mythology was Janus, the Roman god of beginnings. His image, often seen at the gates of cities, had two faces on one head. One face looked to the city within, while the other looked outward. The Janus-faced image represents the dual perspectives of life and meaning in life. This implies that we have a responsibility to self and society, that is, the world within us, and that of other in the outside world. Often the needs, values and expectations of the outside world conflicts with the personal.

Balancing internal and external expectations and meaning in life helps to see the right way to undertake life's journey. This requires balancing *intrapersonal, interpersonal and extra personal interests.*

Intrapersonal interests are interest that comes from within us as individuals, our own self-interest, for example, when you want to be a medical practitioner or lawyer or teacher, and have some particular values you personally hold dear that you do not like to compromise. *Interpersonal* interests are the expectations between you and your direct relationships with others. For example, what your friend(s) or spouse expect from you (a friend expects you to favour him/her or give him or her preferential treatment that may go against your values or lend him/her money you have kept for a particular purpose for yourself. *Extrapersonal* interests on the other hand, are the expectations that society has for us. For example, good citizenship behaviours, obeying the law, or conversely, being part of an organization that expects you to put profit over health and safety of consumers. How you balance these three interests determines your ability to see the right way.

Ability to see the right way therefore entails big picture thinking (Vision and purpose), thinking beyond the immediate situation, and seeing future consequences of your action or decision. It also requires focus on the big-picture so that you are not easily swayed by the "trivial-many", and discipline to values and principles as well as ethical and creative thinking. Ethical and creative thinking helps to assess the consequences and to navigate the traps and contours of life's journey smoothly. Creative thinking is required for solving problems which may come up on the way.

Ethical thinking, in my opinion, is prudence about what is ultimately best or expedient under a given circumstance, whether considered right or wrong. Not all that is logical, right or acceptable, is expedient or prudent. Expedience is that which services the best intentions and purposes and reduces harm to the greater majority. It is more than just what is temporarily good for us as individuals alone.

To make ethical decisions, one must undertake the Alabi Ethical Analysis, which has guided my life by answering the following question:

The moral test: Is it right and acceptable in this context? Do I have doubts about this action or conduct? What are those concerns? Will it keep me thinking afterwards?

The legal test: Is what I am about to do legal? That is, is it in line with procedures or rules that may apply?

The Consequence Test: What will be the consequences of this action or decision? How much harm or good will it cause, and to whom?

Test of Justification: Can I justify my actions, and will that justification be acceptable?

The Interest Test: What is my own interest in this situation or case? How will the consequences affect me and others? What if I put myself in the other people's situation, how would I feel?

Publicity Test: Should my actions or decisions be made public? How would I feel about it? Will I be pleased or proud, and can I boldly associate with it? However, it is important that we do not allow the publicity test to limit our ability to take bold and courageous actions that could bring change and benefit for the greater good.

Sifting through these questions may help us see the right way.

SUMMARY OF SEEING THE RIGHT WAY

One key principle to success is the way and knowing the right way. To know the way, we need to know our purpose and vision in life. I trust that as you identify your purpose and mission in life, your values and principles, your vision of where you want to be, you will know the ways to your destination. Then, by applying big picture thinking, ethical thinking, focus, discipline, and downplaying your ego, you will be able to see the right way and have the power to go on the right ways towards your life's journey. Beware of the easy ways, as often they may be the wrong way and lead you away from the goal and purpose. Do not make the journey a lonely one. Get a sanctuary to help you change your fears and dilemmas into hope, so you can see the right way more clearly.

This chapter is dedicated to Joshua Alabi Jnr., who inspired the title of the chapter when I asked him what he thought makes a man successful or great.

CHAPTER 7

PERSONAL LEADERSHIP PRINCIPLE 6: OVERCOME THE ANTI-PROGRESSIVE FORCES THAT SLOW PERSONAL PROGRESS

Life is 10% what happens to you and 90% how you respond to it. - Charles R. Swindoll[58]

Groucho Marx said "Each morning when I open my eyes, I say to myself: I, not events, have the power to make me happy or unhappy today. I can choose which it shall be. Yesterday is dead, tomorrow hasn't arrived yet. I have just one day, today, and I'm going to be happy in it." Though I appreciate the wisdom in this quote, I do not completely agree that we have the power to make ourselves happy or unhappy every day, because we do not control incidents, accidents, and uncertainties in life. However, I still believe that no matter what the situation may be, we choose our responses to every situation.

Notwithstanding uncertainties and what we do not control, our *state of mind, attitude, and the way we spend, use or invest our time,* goes a long way to influence our outcomes.

---

[58] Charles Swindoll, 2014 Author of the Grace Awaekening, https://www.goodreads.com/author/quotes/5139.Charles_R_Swindoll, retrieved May 11th, 2021.

When it comes to why some succeed, while others fail, many often think it has to do with hard work, luck, discipline, where you come from, who your parents are, the surrounding wealth, or qualifications, or circumstances that push you to crave for success. Indeed, all these may play a role in your success depending on how you use the opportunities that nature gifts to you. However, I have identified four main factors that I believe undermine personal success and progress. These are:

- ignorance
- the blame game
- the dependency syndrome.
- Religion

IGNORANCE

In life, our actions are informed largely by what we know, the information we have at any given time, our interests, our expectations and our values. You are what you think, know, and do. The difference between a truly educated person and an uneducated person lies in the knowledge and information available to them and how they put the knowledge and information they have to use. That is why there are a lot of educated illiterates because the knowledge they have do not work for them. It is said that when an axe is dull and one does not sharpen the edge, one must use more strength when swinging the tool. But wisdom brings success[59]. That is why people who lack the requisite knowledge, competence, or information use more strength and resources, but often fail to be as competitive as a person with more useful and applied knowledge and the right information. Note that knowledge is not only acquired from school or academic education, but everyday life as well.

There are also people with knowledge but lack the needed abilities, such people often need to rely on others or the fruits of other people's knowledge. Knowledge, information, abilities and understanding must work for the possessor. If you have Knowledge, it must produce innovation, technology, products, services and peace. Most importantly, we need to apply our

---

[59]   The Bible, Ecclesiastes 10:10, NKJV.

knowledge to develop in our own way. Knowledge must result in creativity, value addition, and innovation, which are prerequisites for development. To get to your destination, you need light to help you navigate safely, that light is the knowledge, information, abilities and understanding you have at any given time. Look around and you will find a marked difference between people who have knowledge, information and understanding working for them, and you will see the difference between them and those who lack knowledge, information, understanding and abilities. When a person does not have the requisite knowledge, information abilities and understanding, what will work for them? Ignorance is a cancer, which can be cured by acquiring useful and applied knowledge and information.

THE BLAME GAME

The blame game is about looking for someone or something to blame for your situation anytime things do not go well. People can have either an internal or external locus of control. People with an internal locus of control believe that they are responsible for their life, and the outcomes of their choices. On the other hand, people with an external locus of control (people who believe external forces control the outcomes of their lives) often feel they do not have control over the achievement of their goals, and therefore they are not psychologically ready to accept and deal with the consequences of their actions without shifting blame. They often believe that some invincible forces are responsible for the outcomes of their choices, or it is fate. People with an external locus of control therefore try to push blame on one thing or the other for their predicaments. It is quite a cultural influence on whether to either push ourselves to take responsibility and see ourselves as part of the problem, or shift blame to others. In Africa, our culture pushes us more towards an external locus of control thereby shifting blame for our development without considering how much our own attitudes have contributed to our development. For example, in Africa, we tend to blame our developmental slowness and poverty on colonialism and imperialism because it is believed that our current underdevelopment has been caused by imperialism fuelled by colonialism and the slave trade. However, many of Africa's resources were untapped before the arrival of the colonial masters and slave trade. Prior to the arrival of the slave merchants, what was Africa doing with the resources? Simply put, Africa was either unaware or ignorant of most of its resources and /or what to use them for. For example, our gold, diamonds, and oil were largely untapped before the slave merchants arrived. So why do we blame the slave masters for coming to take our gold and giving us mirrors and beads in return?

In 2006, I was in Brussels with a group of professors from different African countries. For most of us, that was our first time in Brussels, so we were very much impressed by the Grand Plaza. During the course of our meeting, we argued about how the buildings were created after looking at the date inscribed on the plaque. One professor remarked, "I don't understand why we credit these people and compare them with Africans. Have you all forgotten that it was our great-grandparents who were hauled from Africa in the most demeaning manner to come build this entire so-called Grand Plaza? I said, "Bravo." But I had some questions. Though I disagree with the demeaning manner in which some of our forebearers were hauled as slaves to Europe and America, did the slaves who built Europe, build similar cities and grand plazas in Africa before they were hauled to Europe or the United States? Why not? Because they were not strategic or were ignorant of the resources. Our great-grandparents had no vision or plans to do anything more than what supported daily living, that is eating, building basic thatched-roof huts to rest body and soul at the end of each day, drumming and dancing, and procreating. And with this they were very contented.

The slave merchants, on the other hand, had a vision, had a plan to build great cities, and needed to mobilize resources. They realized they could mobilize some of the resources they required from Africa, so they came and, lo and behold, found more resources than they had anticipated, along with cheap labour and mineral and oil resources. The results were a great success for them.

Let's consider that coming to Africa to get the slaves was part of the slave merchants' strategy to mobilize the needed resources. However, let us also remind ourselves that resources alone do not turn themselves into added value. Leadership and prudent management is what makes the difference, so why do we blame others. Those slave merchants realised early enough that they have to work and fight for their own development, that only they can create their destinies and the destinies of their future generations. They need not blame others for their situation.

Unfortunately, those of us who were left behind have not made much of a difference, yet we are always blaming our situation on the powers that be, the invincible hands that decide what we should or should not be doing. It is said that no one can make you feel inferior without your permission. We have made ourselves inferior to every other race by our own conduct and value system. We must collectively make a real effort to wake ourselves from our slumber right now and start living so we can make the life we want and leave better legacies behind for future generations. As Africans, we, and only we, are responsible for our development and growth.

Opportunities abound around us, but we hardly identify or take advantage of them. We may have seen several examples of successful people who had to start small, and with focus, dedication, discipline and perseverance made it to global recognition. The continent is plagued with corruption, malnutrition, underdevelopment, squalor, and an overall poor quality of life, though we are making gradual steps towards improvement. Could these conditions be blamed on colonialism or imperialism? Could we by ourselves determine to keep our cities clean, produce enough to feed ourselves and sell some to others, could we decide to cut corruption and focus on using our resources to build our cities and institutions? Can we improve our situation if we stop blaming others and instead identify the true culprits, ourselves, and focus on how to improve our conditions? We need to stop blaming the world for who and what we are. In a practical self-guide like this book, I like to cite people who turned their situations around, so permit me to quote Oprah Winfrey who observed, "The greatest discovery of all time is that a person can change his future by merely changing his attitude." Stop the blame and take responsibility for your own progress.

THE DEPENDENCY SYNDROME

The Bible says in Galatians 4:1, "In so long as the child remains a child, there is no difference between that child and a slave." Children generally depend on others for survival. Therefore, those who overly depend on others for survival are like children and they may be like slaves to those they depend on.

In the book of Proverbs 22: 2 &7 of the Bible, it is stated, "rich and poor have this in common: the Lord is the Maker of them all"... the rich rule over the poor, and the borrower is a slave to the lender."[60] Let us make a clear distinction between interdependence and overdependence. Interdependence is a concept relating to social interactions and relationships that focus on how those involved depend on each other for survival and growth. Overdependence is the excessive reliance on others in a donor-receiver relationship that leaves the recipient at the mercy of the donor. When the donor fails, the receiver blames. The issue here is overdependence and not interdependence, the latter of which is required for accelerated growth. In fact, interdependence is one of the secrets to living smart and being successful.

When you put your breadbasket at the mercy of others who also have their priorities, their priorities will become your priority. If you want someone to help you, you have to be ready to honour the dictates of the helper. Why should we call the conditions of receiving help manipulative? It is only logical to do so.

To be successful, you need to learn to be self-reliant. To be self-reliant, you need to offer something of value to the world and the world will reward you for what you give it.

We need to take our destiny into our own hands and be responsible for our actions and inactions. For as long as we continue to be overdependent, we should be prepared to be treated either as children, who should be told what to do, or as slaves.

Many believe that external forces beyond their control regulate their situation.

A sad mistake is that often in the attempt to emancipate themselves from the insidious dependency syndrome, they blame others by saying "you did not help me, that is what I call the "You Syndrome". There is the pattern of You Syndrome people concurrently thinking they must have independence. Yes, independence is very important and necessary for the exercise of sovereignty and freedom of choice, and it is the only thing

---

[60]   The New International Version (NIV)

that should not be taken from humankind, because human beings should have the power to choose their attitude in a given situation. However, the amateur emancipated mind learns to use the word *I*. Performers say, "I am responsible," because they learn to take responsibility for their actions or inactions or their situation. Nonetheless, performance and responsibility alone are not enough for success and growth in such a competitive world, where resources are not equally or evenly distributed. Learning to say "I" and taking responsibility is certainly a better path than playing the blame game. However, overstretching the limits of I and standing alone has its own problems, which may include unreasonable toil to achieve little, because no individual is an island. The fully emancipated mind therefore says "we". Smart people know the power of we, of team spirit, of collaboration and partnership. You need partnerships to succeed. Working with those who have gone ahead of you is a smart way to achieve your goals. It is often said that when a dwarf stands on the shoulders of a giant, the dwarf can see as much as the giant sees, if not more. We need to reinvent our thinking and attitude if we wish to learn from those who have gone ahead of us through partnerships and networks – not begging. If you want to start a business as an entrepreneur who does not have anyone to help, learn to collaborate with others.

You are a great potential and hope. There is indeed much energy in you, activate it now by rising to use what is in you, what you have and your networks to help you achieve what you desire. Stop the over dependence now and explore interdependence.

RELIGION AND SUCCESS

In 1843, Karl Marx observed that: "Religion is the sigh of the oppressed creature, the heart of a heartless world, and the soul of soulless conditions. It is the opium of the people."[61] However, Marx distinguished between spirituality and religion and observed further that he did not object to a spiritual life, which he thought was necessary. In the "Wages of Labour" of the Economic and Philosophic Manuscripts of 1844, Marx

---

[61] Raines, John. 2002. "Introduction". *Marx on Religion* (Marx, Karl). Philadelphia: Temple University Press. Page 5-6.

wrote: "To develop in greater spiritual freedom, a people must break their bondage to their bodily needs, they must cease to be the slaves of the body, they must, above all, have time at their disposal for spiritual creative activity and spiritual enjoyment."[62] In the Marxist–Leninist interpretation, modern religions and churches are generally considered as "organs of bourgeois reaction" used for "the exploitation and the stupefaction of the working class." In my opinion, religion is like a double-edged knife, it could be useful for success when used as networking for social capital and exhortation and can be a constraint to success when it caps freedom of thought, curiosity and action.

Religion in Africa is a mix of inheritance from three major sources: the African traditional belief system, and the legacies of Christianity and Islam. Religion affects development in Africa in the sense that, generally, Africans tend to lean more on fate than on faith. Many things that happens could be considered fate because people have little or no faith that bigger and better things will happen. So, when people's lack of discipline produces undesired results, it is considered fate. This notion of fate often ignites and consolidates the tendency to accept any situation. The idea of accepting undesirable conditions or situations because they are fated, and we have little control over fate, does not promote and support the need for change and responsibility. Fate, therefore, contributes to our development as a people. This notion of fate needs to be deprogrammed from the minds of the African people if we are to improve our pursuit for development, which requires the need to accept responsibility for our actions and inactions. Excellence comes from consistent outstanding performance. In a situation where performance is ad hoc and not well planned because it is dependent on fate, outcomes are often ambiguous and unpredictable, and any results are accepted as fate. As a consequence of this belief system, excellence could hardly manifest across Africa south of the Sahara, although there are some exceptions. Emancipate yourself from religious bondage and consciously, experience the power of spirituality for your personal success. This concept of spirituality is further discussed in Chapter 13.

---

[62] Shippen, Nichole Marie (2014). *Decolonizing Time: Work, Leisure, and Freedom* (illustrated ed.). New York: Springer. ISBN 9781137354020.

The Need for a Paradigm Shift in How we Perceive Ourselves

As the legendary singer, songwriter, and guitarist Bob Marley once cautioned, we need to "Emancipate ourselves from mental slavery and none but ourselves can free our own minds." Development of ourselves and success begins in our minds. If our minds are correctly understood, then our vision will be clear, and our attitude will be right to achieve the development and success we need. It is important for us in Africa to realize that we enslaved ourselves before we were enslaved, and now we are still enslaved by our own thinking and mind-set.

To overturn this mind-set requires a radical transformation of what we perceive as success. Success should not be perceived as the attainment of riches or higher qualifications, but contribution to development and country.

Again, Bob Marley, in verse two of his song "The Rat Race," said, "In the abundance of water, the fool is thirsty." Why should you be poor in Africa, with its abundance of resources? As Zig Ziglar notes "Your attitude, not your aptitude, will determine your altitude." When you start with a positive attitude, you are likely to end on a positive note. Stop nagging, stop blaming others, make a firm decision to develop yourself and others will appreciate the value in you. Accordingly, it is only us who can free our minds from the bondage of inferiority and move in the direction of success. Education should be concerned with how learning takes place, how knowledge is imparted, and how education can be used to assist individuals and groups in overcoming mental slavery, unleashing their potential, and resolving the critical problem of personal and collective success

CHAPTER 8

PERSONAL LEADERSHIP PRINCIPLE SEVEN

LET FATE, FAITH, WORKS, AND LUCK WORK TOWARDS YOUR SUCCESS

The best place to succeed is where you are with
what you have. - Charles M. Schwab

How do fate, faith, work, and luck contribute to success?

No one chooses where they are born or who their parents are. However, where you are born and who your parents are can influence your success in life, that is fate. Fate is a compilation of situations that you cannot control. Fate can therefore be a positive encounter or a negative encounter. Some people call positive fate encounters good luck and negative fate encounters bad luck. Many people believe that a lot of the things that come their way is fated, and therefore, what will be will be. For some people your fate is your destiny and therefore such people have little control over life's outcomes. On the other hand, some people believe that you can change your destiny by redirecting what fate brings to you through faith, work, and the right choices.

On 10th July 2014, I was in a meeting with six other academics, mostly Professors, and were discussing the subject of '*Nature or Nurture* and how these two influences who and what we are'. One of the Professors asked us, 'to what extent do you think our lives are influenced by our personality, where we are born, and the environment that nurtured us'? The responses were amazing. The majority indicated that who and what we are comes more from nature, and only about 20-25% of what we are comes from nurture. I was amazed because I have held the belief that we are more of what we and society makes of us than what nature makes of us. So I tended to disagree with them, and that led to a debate and analysis of the issues. We began to analyse each concept one after the other.

One Professor remarked "I tell you, at the age of two, my daughter's attitude was already cast in certain ways, and she has not changed much since that time, she is now seventeen." This was in support of the nature (fate) argument. Another professor with a medical background opined that "it is all about our aim or goal in life and the sacrifices we make." He added, "if we feel hungry enough to want to change our situation, no matter how bad it is, we can do it, we only need to be focused. He continued, "It is said in Africa that when you look in the bottle with both eyes, you will miss the target. I tell you, if you want to achieve everything, be everything to everyone, you will assert nothing, and if you do not know what you want to achieve, you will not achieve anything. Success requires determination to reach one's goals and ability to fight the battles that come with reaching your goals. Look at me, he continued, I was born in a village to illiterate parents, but as I grew and noted the benefit of school, I was determined to work hard, and go through school. Today, I am here with all of you who had different backgrounds. My destiny was not capped by who my parents were and where I was born, but achieved through hard work, faith and focus.

Others argued that gifts and talents endowed to people by nature determines whether you will succeed in a particular field or not. However, the counterargument to this is that talent and gifts are nothing if they are not turned into abilities. Turning talents or natural gifts into abilities requires efforts and sacrifices for them to yield results. At this point, the proponent of the abilities over talents and gifts, gave the example of some known tennis icons, Serena and Venessa Williams, who are both world tennis stars. These ladies, according to what he had read, grew up in rather disadvantaged circumstances. They had talents which were natural, but their talents did not make them stars, rather it was their hard work, focus, and discipline that made them the iconic world champions they are today.

One other Professor from Ghana, in support of the nature argument, cited Abedi Ayew Pele and his sons Jordan and Andrea Ayew all world class footballers as support for the nature arguement. He argued that the talent they have is genetically derived, and that others could focus and train even harder than the Abede family but may not get their kind of results. By now, the discussion was shifting more in favour of nurture. For me, it was getting more in favour of abilities and attitude, which favours, nurturing. By the end of the discussion, it was clear that though nature (people's personalities, gifts and talents) plays an important role, success and life's outcomes are more from nurturing than nature. Nurturing requires a conscious effort of choices, actions, behaviours and attitudes, though fate counts to a large extent. Nurturing is an outcome of environmental influences, work and faith, not fate or luck. This is why I agree with Charles M. Schwab when he says, *"The best place to succeed is where you are with what you have."*

FATE

For the Professors discussing the issue of nature and nurture, your birth, **your genotype**, your personality, where you were born, where you grew up, and all the things that you do not have control over, represent your fate. In the end, we agreed that though there are many things that come to us in life, which we do not have control over, our choices and actions can change the influences of fate on the outcomes of our lives.

Faith on the other hand, is how we visualize who we are and what we want, and the belief that we can make it happen. That *"can do"* belief is what I call faith. Faith is actually the way we direct our thoughts, visualize the outcome of those thoughts and make them happen. Faith is thought in action. Our faith reflects how we act on the thoughts we hold and work towards the actualization of those thoughts. You cannot exercise faith without thoughts, visualization and action. Thought and visualization without action is wishful thinking.

Dan Robey, an internet blogger on Positive Habits, wrote a piece entitled '*This Little Boy "Visualized" An Empire*'. [63] I found that true story about the power of visualization amazing. This is the piece:

Many, many years ago, a young boy chanced to pass by a newspaper publishing office. Intrigued by what could be happening inside, he stopped and peeped through the window and became fascinated by what he saw in the office. The actions of the chief editor of the newspaper stirred something in him. The young boy was astonished as the editor screamed orders at the employees around him. The boy realised the power that the chief editor possessed, and how the entire newspaper enterprise seemed to revolve around him. The young boy began to visualize himself as that editor.

Every day he pictured himself as the editor of that newspaper; he dreamed about it at night. He created a detailed vision in his mind of himself in that editor's chair just as I had visualized myself in St. Mary's Secondary School, Korle Gonno Accra in 1987. It was almost like he had created a vivid colour movie that he played back in his mind every night. This is the most important part of this story. The movie that this young boy played in his mind every night slowly began to manifest itself in the real world. The young boy got a part-time job at a newspaper publishing company. The part-time job turned into a full-time job as an editor.

Who was that young boy? His name was Roger Ferger. Not only did he become the editor of a large newspaper, but he also eventually went on to become the owner and publisher of the Cincinnati Inquirer, one of the largest newspaper empires in the United States today.

Are you visualizing who you want to become? What is your Positive Visualization? It can be summarized in this one statement: "We were created in the image of our creator; therefore, we are creators." Think about this statement very carefully. We create our world. Everything that you, or anyone else has done since the beginning of time, began first with a thought. If you look back at the careers of successful people, you will find that almost every one of them first visualized who they wanted to be long before they actually achieved success. But their success was not only because they thought and planned, but because they took the right actions.

---

63   Dan Robey

Pause and think about who you want to be and what you want to accomplish in your life in the next few years. You may be wishing for a new career, to go back to school, graduate with honours, or you may have a health and fitness goal. You may want to spend more time with loved ones, or tour the world, or start a new business, or buy that dream house you always wanted. Create a wish list, turn it into a to-do list, and write strategies about how to accomplish them year by year. Ensure that your list is somewhere you can read it every day and visualize the accomplishment of the goals on your list.

Create a detailed movie in your mind of the 'new you' that you want to be. Be very detailed, if your goal was an honours degree or a new career, picture yourself holding the certificate or walking into the office or your new company as an entrepreneur. Picture every detail, the colour and inscriptions on the certificate, the office set up and ambiance, or the production and service to customers in the case of an entrepreneur. If your goal is a promotion, picture yourself in that new office, believe it with all your heart as if it were already real. No matter what your goals are, visualize them every day. Now, how many times have you not visualized achieving something? Did it always happen? Why not? ***Visualization without action is wishful thinking***. Faith fills our souls with strong desires and passion. It strengthens us so we can reach our goals and the things we visualize through our actions.

Continuing my conversation with the professors, we considered whether fate played a role for the boy (Roger Ferger) when he walked past that window that day. Or what if he did not peep through the window, which is considered ill-mannered? Would he have seen the editor? What if the editor was not in that position on that day? Then one said, "that is fate for you!" Another replied, "no not fate, luck!" But for luck, would he have seen the editor that day? "Tell me" he continued, "would he have seen the same editor in a different environment if he were to be elsewhere, or if he did not go that way?" The third Professor replied gently, "it is only bad luck that happens by accident. Good luck is when preparation meets opportunity. This guy subconsciously wanted to succeed." Another person may have seen this scene – a man shouting at others – and the experience would have no significance, he will have forgotten it a minute after the encounter. However, this encounter became a source of inspiration and a target for this young man. He began to think about it. It did not just occupy his thoughts, he began to visualize himself in that chair – faith in action. He later took action and got a job in a newspaper company. What if he had not responded the way he did through his actions, would there have been a Cincinnati Inquirer? This boy could have gone past without peering. He might not have used his observation in any meaningful way. However, his fate, faith, thoughts and actions came together to offer him luck and success.

Benjamin Desrearli, a two-time Prime Minister of Britain, and the first foreigner to be Britain's Prime Minister, once said, the secret of success is for a man to be ready for his time when it comes. When we are not ready for our time through earlier thoughts and preparation, great opportunities will always elude us. So I believe, it is not so much about where we are born, our nationality, or the environment in which we grew up in, but it is our thoughts, attitudes and actions that make the difference. Below is an extract that exemplifies this belief:

Malala Yousafzai was an unlikely leader. In 2012, at age 15, the Pakistani girl survived a Taliban assassination attempt for her outspoken advocacy supporting education for girls. One of the three bullets fired pierced her forehead and travelled down into her shoulder, leaving her in critical condition in the days following. Although Malala entered the hospital as an unknown, she emerged as a global figure, positioned for leadership on the international stage. Her passion, vigilance, and dedication to the cause of equal education secured her place in history and inspired millions of others to support her efforts. Malala received the first National Youth Peace Prize and was nominated in 2013 and 2014 for the Nobel Peace Prize. Malala was ready and prepared to grab the opportunity to do what she believed in. Fate hit her hard, but her faith kept her alive and her dreams burning. In her words, she said "fate can shoot a body but not my dreams." Her Faith sustained the dreams and brought them to life. It is amazing that our thoughts alone can be responsible for such a powerful result. The fact is that we are the product of what goes on in our minds. Yet many of us think negatively about our prospects, our dreams, and our ambitions. We allow the reality of our day-to-day existence to get us down. We become disconnected from our path and our ambitions. We become discouraged and lose our motivation. It is the extraordinary leader who has the ability to see past what "is" and to envision what "may be." Although most people have sight, it is a select few who have vision.

Perhaps you've heard a version of "The Starfish Thrower" experience and enlightenment by author and philosopher Loren Eiseley: One day, an older man was walking on the beach along the shoreline. As he looked down the beach, he saw a young man moving deliberately, yet gracefully, up and down; up and down. As he got closer, he saw that the young man was reaching down into the sand, picking up something, and very gently throwing it into the ocean. As he got closer, he called out, "Good morning! What are you doing?" The young man paused, looked up and replied, "Throwing starfish into the ocean." The older man asked, "Why are you throwing starfish into the ocean?" The young man answered, "The sun is up and the tide is going out. And if I don't throw them in they'll die." The older man paused and said, "But young man, don't you realize that there are miles and miles of beach and starfish all along it. You can't possibly make a difference!" The young man listened politely, nodded his head and continued on as before. He bent down, picked up another starfish and threw it past the breaking waves into the sea and said, "It made a difference for that one!" It is that type of vision that allows one to see beyond the current circumstances and move into the realm of possibility, defying the odds in pursuit of a worthy goal.

Much like the young man on the beach, everyone has the power to make a difference through one connection at a time. Yes, there will be naysayers and detractors, and there will be moments when the "beach" of doing business seems endless and ineffective; yet each connection holds the same opportunity and potential as the starfish that received a new start. Never underestimate the impact and power of managing relationships – or minimize the fact that one single connection can make all the difference in the world.

Ray Kroc, the businessman who built the international McDonald's fast-food restaurant empire, was perhaps one of the most savvy and successful businessmen that the world has seen. He shared these words that we all can learn from: "Happiness is not a tangible thing, it's a by-product—a by-product of achievement. Achievement must be made against the possibility of failure, against the risk of defeat. It is no achievement to walk a tightrope laid flat on the floor. Where there is no risk, there can be no pride in achievement and, consequently, no happiness. The only way we can advance is by going forward, individually and collectively, in the spirit of the pioneer. We must take the risks involved in our free enterprise system. This is the only way in the world to economic freedom. There is no other way" (Kroc, 204-205)[64].

Whether you are a catalyst for change as the beacon from a lighthouse or the subtle, yet seismic shift in the status quo, shining light as a lantern in your personal sphere of the world, I invite, encourage, and challenge you to do the thing that you were created to do. Fate, faith and work therefore work together to produce luck.

---

[64] Ray Kroc, 1992, Grinding it Out: The Making of Mcdonalds, Martins Press https://www.goodreads.com/work/quotes/487021, Retrieved June 2021

PART 2

PUTTING IT ALL TOGETHER - THE FOUR CAPITALS OF SUCCESS

CHAPTER 9

PUTTING IT ALL TOGETHER - THE FOUR CAPITALS OF SUCCESS

To the Heart of the Matter

So far, we have seen the discussions about the seven personal leadership principles mentioned in this book. These include knowing yourself, self-direction, self-regulation and control, the way and the power to see the right way, overcoming the anti-progress forces, Mastering the your quotients (IQ, KQ, EQ, XQ, SQ, AQ, and PQ), examples of success stories, arguments about fate, faith and work, and we have discussed the anti-progress forces. Putting all of these together I synthesized the four capitals for personal success. These are:

- Personal Capital
- Human Capital
- Social Capital
- Spiritual Capital

This part of the book looks at each of the four capitals, starting with a discussion of the concept of personal success.

WHAT IS PERSONAL SUCCESS?

When I set out to write this book, I wondered if I was not trying to open a Pandora's box because success is difficult to define. I also wondered whether there is a particular set of traits, skills, practices which can be used as a formula for success? Obviously, different routes can lead to success. No one particular set of behaviours or principles and practices could provide definitive predictive models for success because life is organic and often does not end up exactly where we expect it to be. In short, there is no science for the journey of life, the destination by which we define success or failure. Not IQ, KQ nor EQ, SQ, AQ, nor XQ can make us end up exactly where we expect to be. Good luck counts, but not without the bad. Fate may count, but not without faith. Knowledge may count, but not without an appreciation of what we do not know. Urgency counts, but not without patience. Execution counts, but not without adversity. But one thing is also clear, the rich and the poor have one thing in common, they are all humans and creations of God. So what sets them apart? Is it the gifts they have from birth, the abilities they develop, where they are born or who their parents are? I have seen men and women from humble beginnings become prominent, influential or wealthy. I have seen men who achieved wealth, but the process of acquiring their wealth destroyed them. I have seen men and women born with golden spoons in their mouths, who ended up as servants because they could not replicate the achievements and values of their parents or exemplify the family they came from. I have seen men and women from wealthy and very esteemed families, lifting the banner of their roots even higher. I have seen men and women who may not be exceedingly wealthy, but their contributions, imprinted their names not only in the sands of time but in the hearts of people. Which of these would you describe as successful or unsuccessful?

I have also seen men and women strive and struggle to cross the Mediterranean in the search of a better life, only to plunge themselves into free will servitude. I have seen men and women struggle to gain citizenship of Europe, America, Canada, Australia among others. Some have also pursued knowledge and qualifications to the peril of other social aspects of life. Some become successful others do not. But in all of these, would we say they found fulfilment, true happiness, freedom, peace and soundness of mind? Why and why not? Your answers may be as good as mine.

The Concept of Success Explained

Success is an elusive concept because it means different things to different people. For some it is about being fulfilled, happy, safe, healthy, loved, free, and of sound mind and sound environment. For me success is the ability to reach your goals in life in a way that makes you fulfilled, happy, peaceful and of sound mind whatever, those goals may be. An individual's mission in life has unique purpose and goals, and consequently, so is their definition of success unique to them. To be successful means you know why you exist and do all that it takes to make that purpose and your mission in life fulfilled in a manner that brings you joy, happiness, peace of mind and love. Success is not mere material accumulation like houses, cars, jewellery, degrees and accolades, or power and influence. It can encompass all of those material acquisitions mentioned, but mere possession of these material acquisitions does not equate to success. Material acquisitions should be by-products of true success gained through the fulfilment of your purpose, goals or aspiration, in a way that makes you fulfilled, happy and peaceful because your actions or inaction helped someone and made them happy too. It is important to note that we can be fulfilled, and not happy and peaceful, so mere fulfilment of goals and aspirations is not success.

Ted Kaczynski, the Hermit of Harvard, for example, fulfilled his mission to plant bombs, but did that bring him joy and peace? His bombs killed three people and injured 29 others between 1978 and 1995. Theodore John Kaczynski was arrested at his one-room, wooden cabin near Lincoln, Montana on April 3, 1996 where he had confined himself, more or less as a fugitive.

Was Theodore of sound mind at the time, was he happy, did he enjoy peace, was he free, was he generally loved and was he in a safe environment?

In an article by William Claiborne in a Washington Post special report on the Unabomber, Ted Kaczynski was identified by the FBI as the Unabomber, implicated in three murders and 16 bombings, and described as someone with feelings of inferiority. By "feelings of inferiority" we mean not only inferiority feelings in the strict sense, but a whole spectrum of related traits, low self-esteem, feelings of powerlessness, depressive tendencies, defeatism, guilt, self-hatred, etc."[65] Kaczynski achieved his aspiration and goal to plant bombs, but he was not fulfilled, and therefore unsuccessful.

PABLO ESCOBAR

Pablo Emilio Escobar Gaviria, also known as El Patron, was a Colombian drug lord and narcoterrorist who established the Medellín Cartel as sole leader. Generally acknowledged as "The King of Cocaine," Escobar is believed to be the wealthiest criminal in history, having amassed an estimated net worth of US$30 billion by the time of his death, equivalent to $59 billion as of 2019. His drug cartel monopolized the cocaine trade into the United States in the 1980s and early 1990s.[66,67]

Escobar is reported to have studied very briefly at Universidad Autónoma Latinoamericana of Medellín but left without graduating. He preferred to start building his criminal empire, selling banned cigarettes, fake lottery tickets, and stolen vehicles. Poised to make his mark in the sands of time, Escobar began to work for various drug smugglers in the early 70s, often holding people for ransom. This was the training ground where Escobar honed his craft and became well-equipped to beat his predecessors and masters from whom he had learnt.

Having mastered his craft from his experiences on the job, Escobar founded the Medellín Cartel in 1976. With his new cartel, he started supplying powder cocaine, and established the first smuggling routes into the United States. Escobar's infiltration into the U.S. generated unusual

---

[65] Washington post, special report on the Unabomber https://www.washingtonpost.com/wp-srv/national/longterm/unabomber/manifesto.text.htm, Friday, August 21, 1998; Page A02

[66] "10 facts reveal the absurdity of Pablo Escobar's wealth". *Business Insider.* Retrieved 28 July 2018.

[67] "Here's How Rich Pablo Escobar Would Be If He Was Alive Today". *UNILAD.* 13 September 2016. Archived from the original on 29 July 2018. Retrieved 28 July 2018.

demand for cocaine and by the 1980s it was estimated that Escobar led monthly shipments of 70 to 80 tons of cocaine into the US from Colombia. As a result, he quickly became one of the richest people in the world.[68] The journey was not easy at all for Escobar. He had to fight a myriad of battles, overcome rival cartels both home and abroad, the crooked police in many of these rival cartels were also hunting him, he led several massacres and the murders of police officers, judges, locals, including innocent pedestrians, and prominent politicians, making Colombia the murder capital of the world.[69,70]

In 1982, Escobar tested his influence and was elected as an alternate member of the Chamber of Representatives of the Colombian Parliament as part of the Liberal Alternative movement. As a politician, Escobar got involved in community projects such as the construction of houses and football fields, which gained him popularity among the locals of the communities that benefitted from his projects. However, Escobar was criticized by many, including the Colombian and U.S. governments,[71] who pursued his arrest.

Pablo had achieved his aspirations by rising from a simple and obscure middle class to one of the world's wealthiest businessmen. At the peak of his career, Pablo owned about fifteen aeroplanes, including a Learjet, and six helicopters as well as ranches.[72] Pablo Escobar was killed in his hometown after a nationwide manhunt in 1993 by the Colombian National Police, a day after his 44th birthday. In a book written by Escobar Gaviria, entitled

68 Juan Pablo, 2014, *Pablo Escobar, My Father*. Escobar, St. Martin's Press, New York Page 469, retrieved March 9 2021.
69 Pablo Escobar Gaviria – English Biography – Articles and Notes". ColombiaLink. com. Archived from the original on 8 November 2006. Retrieved 16 March 2011. Cited March 18th 2021
70 *"Pablo Emilio Escobar 1949 – 1993 9 Billion USD – The business of crime – 5 'success' stories"*. MSN. 17 January 2011. Archived from *the original* on 14 July 2011. *Retrieved 16 March 2011.*
71 Karl Penhaul (9 May 2003). "Drug kingpin's killer seeks Colombia office". *Boston Globe*
72 *"Decline of the Medellín Cartel and the Rise of the Cali Mafia"*. U.S. Drug Enforcement Administration. Archived from *the original* on 18 January 2006. *Retrieved 13 February 2010.* And cited 18th March, 2010

My Brother - Pablo Escobar, his brother described how Pablo became infamous before his death.[73]

Was Pablo successful? May be yes, may be no. From my checklist, Pablo may have achieved his goals, but he was not a free man. His wealth killed many people, caused pain to families and destroyed state institutions. On the other hand, he built schools, parks, and many social amenities for the poor in his communities where his legacy is cherished till date. Many poor who benefited from his generosity consider him a saint and pray to him for divine help.[74]

The author Jerrid Grimm observed, "El Patron is not only one of the most successful criminals of all time, but he is one of the most successful entrepreneurs in history. He took an undervalued product to a new market, established production controls, supply chain management and distribution agreements to become one of the wealthiest men in the world. All the while, being repeatedly shot at by his competitors, the police, and the government."[75] What lesson can you learn from Pablo's story? For me, Pablo's story teaches us about a man who achieved his career goals and accumulated wealth through his commitment to his personal goals (Personal Capital), development of his skills and an attitude of bravery and audacity (Human Capital) that his goals required. He also developed the networks (Social Capital) that supported him, and spiritual fortitude that gave him the confidence to press on even in the face of dire consequences (Spiritual Capital). Would you say Pablo was successful or unsuccessful? How does Pablo's achievements relate to the four capitals? We will find out soon.

---

[73] Escobar Gaviria, Roberto (2016). My Brother - Pablo Escobar. Escobar, Inc. ISBN 978-0692706374.

[74] Wallace, Arturo (2 December 2013). "Drug boss Pablo Escobar still divides Colombia". *BBC News*.

[75] Jerrid Grimm, 2nd December 2015, "What you can learn about business from Pablo Escobar" https://www.linkedin.com/in/jerridgrimm/?lipi=urn%3Ali%3Apage%3Ad_flagship3_pulse_read%3BSLfSSw4nSJG3z7fl8DFVbA%3D%3D&licu=urn%3Ali%3Acontrol%3Ad_flagship3_pulse_read-read_profile, Retrieved 18th March, 2021

EXAMPLES OF SOME OF AFRICA'S SUCCESSFUL PEOPLE AND THE FOUR CAPITALS

Success comes in different sizes and shapes, depending on our purpose, goals and aspirations. Maurice Setter notes that "too many people miss the silver lining because they're expecting gold." Many people bypass success in their quest or haste to catch it, simply because their concept of success, makes success itself elude them.

Looking for examples to buttress my points on success, I came across a BBC News publication entitled "**Five inspiring stories of dedication and change in Africa from 2019**".[76] I chose these five success stories because they do not necessary relate to wealth or material accumulation, but to fulfilment, joy and peace.

1. Peter Tabichi

In March 2019, Peter Tabichi was awarded the Global Teacher Prize by a panel of judges in Dubai. Peter received a hero's welcome in Kenya on his return from Dubai after receiving the golden trophy for the world's best teacher.

The joy expressed by Peter's students in celebrating his award was evidence of how much he was appreciated at home. Peter is a modest Franciscan monk who teaches maths and physics and donates much of his salary to support poorer pupils at the rural secondary school in Nakuru county, Kenya. Reflecting on the year, Perter told the BBC that the award was "clear evidence that Africa's young people have a lot of potential to positively transform the world. It has also inspired many people and showed that "teachers play a very important role in bringing the needed change in society through education".

Whereas some are frustrated with their jobs as teachers and are always hoping for a better job somewhere, someday, Peter found beauty and harmony in teaching because he knows his purpose. Peter therefore chose to make meaning with his life through teaching and serving the poor.

---

[76] BBC, December 2019, Five Inspiring Stories Of Dedication And Change In Africa From 2019, https://www.bbc.com/news/world-africa-50782677 retrieved 12the March, 2021

Peter's recognition and award celebrates his contribution, not his money or accolades. Peter's success clearly came from purpose, passion, and dedication to all aspects of Personal Capital, human capital, social and spiritual capital at work.

2. New mother, new Graduate: A case of Determination

The story of the young Ethiopian Almaz Derese, 21, is also inspiring. Derese would not let anything stop her from getting a secondary school certificate. Not pregnancy or labour or childbirth would get in the way of Derese finishing her secondary education.

In June 2019, Derese went into labour shortly before her first exam was due to start. She gave birth to a boy, Yididiya, and then 30 minutes later sat the exam from her hospital bed. Almaz Derese took three exams at the Karl Mettu hospital in western Ethiopia. She told the BBC "Because I was rushing to sit the exam, my labour wasn't difficult at all." In June, Ms Almaz found out she passed with a mark of 75%. The new mother said she did not expect such a good result as she was in pain whilst writing the papers. Derese adds, "During my pregnancy, I was not comfortable sleeping at night, so I used the time to study," she told the BBC. Her success gave her the opportunity to continue and finish secondary school in two more years, and then apply to university. Derese aspires to become an engineer. Derese literally turned her obstacles into an opportunity by learning at night when she could not sleep because of the pregnancy. Tenacity and audacity are what we see here. What is stopping you from pursuing your dreams? Stop the excuses and get into action with phycological preparedness to face the odds. Audacity and Tenacity make the difference for many people, this is a combination of Personal Capital - her personal goals and aspirations, Human Capital - her studies, Social Capital - support from her husband and family, and Spiritual Capital - her tenacity.

3. 'I'm just a messenger': Service is the Purpose of Life

Mr Alfred Brownell, a Liberian lawyer and activist, received the Goldman Environmental Prize for his work in environmental conservation because his advocacy stopped the destruction of 500,000 acres of rainforest in Liberia. Brownell's recognition stemmed from working with local community leaders to document the destruction of forests and farmlands in the south-east of Liberia by palm oil company Golden Veroleum Liberia (GVL). In an interview with the BBC after winning the major environmental prize, Brownell said "I'm just a messenger - the real winners are the communities." As a result of his work, the global certification body, the Roundtable on Sustainable Palm Oil, put a "stop work" order on GVL, freezing any expansion of the palm oil plantations and preventing any further forest clearance. Brownell's success is a demonstration that service and contribution are key measures of success in life. Brownell typifies all the four capitals. His goal to stop the destruction of rain forest Personal Capital, his Human Capital – which is his research and advocacy skills that brought the issues before those with authority, the Social Capital – which is his Goldman team, and the Spiritual Capital – which is the desire to serve the people whose lives depended on it, and save the environment, a course greater than himself.

SOME SUCCESSFUL AFRICAN ENTREPRENEURS

Many complain about their jobs, and lament how they want to change their jobs or start their own jobs. Often, they find excuses about why they are not successful at finding or starting their own Jobs. The excuses include not knowing anyone in a position of authority who could help them, or unsupportive family members, or banks not willing to provide start-up capital. Others hope to find a better life elsewhere, often abroad. Yet there are some successful entrepreneurs in Africa. So how did they do it? To address this question, I stumbled upon a catalogue of some successful entrepreneurs in Africa whose successes had been compiled by John-Paul Iwuoha, an impact entrepreneur, and founder of Smallstarter Africa. John-Paul also co-authored the book 101 Ways To Make Money in Africa. I present here five selected Successful African Entrepreneurs.[77]

---

[77] John-Paul Iwuoha February 22, 2016 How These 10 Super Successful African Entrepreneurs Raised Money To Start Their Businesses, https://www.linkedin. com/pulse/how-10-super-successful-african-entrepreneurs-raised-money-iwuoha/, retrieved 12th March, 2021

Aliko Dangote (Nigeria): Focus and Consistency are Key to Success

Aliko Dangote has emerged as Africa's richest man in 2021 and for the previous ten years, with an estimated worth of $12.1 billion. What made Dangote so successful? Interestingly, Dangote's business success has been built with focus and consistency over the last three decades. The Dangote Group is one of the largest private-sector employers in Nigeria, as well as the most valuable conglomerate in West Africa.[78]

Dangote was born into a wealthy family but did not rely on the already made wealth of the family and choose a life of contentment and satisfaction with the status quo, just as many people born into rich families do. For Dangote, success is about contribution and not mere riches. Dangote was determined to build his own business empire (Vision -Personal Capital) and he did so with glowing success. He spent much of his childhood with his grandfather after the death of his father in 1965. Dangote quickly became interested in the world of business, and once said, "I can remember when I was in primary school, I would go and buy cartons of sweets [sugar boxes] and I would start selling them just to make money. I was so interested in business, even at that time.[79]

At age 21, Dangote graduated from Egypt's Al-Azhar University, considered one of Islam's most prestigious universities. Dangote advanced his education in business to enhance his entrepreneurial potential. He graduated from university in 1977 and got a loan of $3000 from his uncle to start a business in 1978. With this seed money, he started to import rice and sugar at wholesale prices from Thailand and Brazil. His business soon became successful, and he expanded.[17]

In an interview with FORBES Africa journalist Peace Hyde, Dangote gave some advice to the youth, "Dangote has had his fair share of ups and downs. But his advice to young entrepreneurs is having the ability to delay

---

[78] Warren Cassell Jr., Feb 15, 2021, How Did Aliko Dangote Become The Richest Person In Africa?
      https://www.investopedia.com/articles/investing/100615/how-aliko-dangote-became-richest-african.asp#citation-5, Retrieved 12th March, 2021

[79] All Africa. "Nigeria: Aliko Dangote - a Lesson for African Entrepreneurs." Accessed Dec. 19, 2020. https://allafrica.com/stories/201403240379.html, retrieved 12th March, 2021

gratification (EQ) and work hard through tough times (AQ) so they can enjoy the fruits of their labour at a later date," says Hyde.[80,81]

With a conglomerate that currently spreads across Africa, Dangote's impressive fortune was built from very humble beginnings of focus and consistency of actions.

Adii Pienaar (South Africa): Not too Young to Start

Adii Pienaar is the South African co-founder of WooThemes, a tech company recently acquired by US-based online tech giant Automattic, for $30 million. Adii started WooThemes in 2008 at age 23 while he was still attending university. Adii worked as a part-time online freelancer and consultant while working at WooThemes on the side. Using a bootstrapping approach, he ploughed his savings from his earnings into his business. Bootstrapping is a strategy of starting a business with no money or, at least, very little money, and building on little by little. Adii observes, "It is the art of making personal sacrifices, using personal savings and limited financial resources to support a business in its early days".

"When asked how the business started, Adii noted that despite his impressive success with WooThemes, it has not been an easy path. "In 2007, I was doing a lot of WordPress custom design/development work for clients. I was keen to find a passive income source and I wanted to make the roll-out of custom WordPress websites much easier, so I created my first ever "premium" WordPress theme. This theme led to the introductions and subsequent collaboration with my WooThemes co-founders in July 2008". Bootstrappers have a very remarkable fighting spirit and I trust Adii will soon join the list of African Billionaires through focus, consistency and resilience.

---

[80] Peace Hyde, The Forbes Billionaires List: Africa's Billionaires 2020 https://www.cnbcafrica.com/2020/the-forbes-billionaires-list-africas-billionaires-2020/

[81] CNBC Africa, The Forbes Billionaires List: Africa's Billionaires 2021, https://www.cnbcafrica.com/2021/the-forbes-billionaires-list-africas-billionaires-2021/, retrieved 12th March 2021

Fomba Trawally (Liberia): Your Circumstance is no Excuse

Fomba Trawally's is a former refugee who became one of Liberia's richest entrepreneurs. His success is an inspiration. Fomba left school and started selling shower slippers in a wheelbarrow to support his siblings after his mother's death. However, the civil war which started in 1989, forced him to move to The Gambia as a refugee. By the end of 1991, Fomba returned home with as little as $25, which he had saved, and $120 that he got from a friend to start his new business, Kumba Beindu and Sons, that dealt in rubber slippers (flip-flops). Flip Flops were in high demand at the time. Fomba notes "In just one year, we were able to grow up to $3,000, and now we have businesses all around the country," he told the BBC's series, African Dream. Kumba Beindu and Sons have now diversified into other plastic products and cosmetics from countries such as China, the United States, Turkey, and neighbouring Ivory Coast. In 2010, Trawally transitioned from being an importer to a manufacturer, when he set up National Toiletries Incorporated, Liberia's first paper and toiletry products manufacturing company, with an annual sale that has crossed the $1 million mark. In life, your circumstance may be a constraint, but not a limitation, with determination and focus you can succeed.

Bethlehem Tilahun Alemu (Ethiopia): Where there is a Will there must be a Way

Bethlehem Tilahun is a young woman with an inspiring success story that featured on Forbes, the BBC and CNN. Forbes described Bethlehem as 'One of The World's Most Powerful Women'.

"Bethlehem Alemu grew up in a poor village in the suburbs of Addis Ababa, Ethiopia. She started SoleRebels, one of Africa's most popular and fastest-growing eco-friendly footwear brands in the world, with products made from only recycled materials. Her footware has been sold in over 50 countries across the world, including the USA, Canada, Japan and Switzerland, with an annual revenue in excess of $1 million.

Bethlehem started with about $10,000 seed capital she raised from family and relatives in 2004. She has just launched "Republic of Leather", a new business that trades in luxury leather products like bags, belts, and other non-footwear leather accessories. Evidently, where you come from does not matter, it is what you have to offer the world and your community, and how you offer it that makes the difference. Where there is a will, there is always a way.

Patrick Ngowi (Tanzania): Age is not a Barrier

Patrick Ngowi, featured by Forbes as one of '10 Young African Millionaires to Watch' is next. Patrick started business at age 19 by selling Chinese made mobile phones. His business has cascaded into one of East Africa's most successful solar energy companies, Helvetic Solar Contractors. Like most success stories, Ngowi's journey has not been easy. He started with a loan of $1,800 from his mother, while a close friend supported his trip to China. In 2013, Helvetic Solar Contractors made more than $5 million in revenue and was valued by KPMG East Africa in 2014 at $15 million.

These success stories teach us about men and women who were determined to make a difference through their thoughts and actions, as well as their focus, discipline and perseverance. The question is, why don't others make it? To provide some answer to this question, refer to the four Anti-Progress Forces, and now the Four Capitals.

CHAPTER 10

PERSONAL CAPITAL: WHO ARE YOU AND WHAT ARE YOU LIVING FOR?

Our attitude toward life determines life's
attitude towards us. — John Mitchell

THE CONCEPT OF PERSONAL CAPITAL

As described earlier, Personal Capital refers to an understanding of self and using that understanding to create a life of fulfilment and success. The more you know and understand yourself, what works for you, and what does not work for you, the higher your Personal Capital. Personal Capital entails *self-awareness, awareness of others, self-direction, self-regulation and control, personal purpose or mission in life, and personal drives or passion.* This requires an awareness of who you are, what makes you different - **personality**, what you exist to do - **purpose**, who you exist to serve - **place**, what drives you - **passion**, your value and what you value – your **price and principles**, and your ability to achieve personal goals - **performance.**

THE SEVEN PS OF PERSONAL CAPITAL

- Personality
- Purpose
- Passion

- Place
- Price
- Principles
- Performance

Personality

Your personality includes how you look, how you behave, and your disposition. It is important to understand that you are unique and so is your purpose and your opportunity to make a difference in life. Tall or short, slim or chubby, light skin, pointed nose, broad nose, long flowy hair, curly kinky short hair, dark skin, fleshy lips or thin lips, skinny legs or thick legs, sharp witted, cunning, fantastic memory, forward thinker, born into poverty, born wealthy, sporty, academic – no one else can ever, ever, be you and your life can never be repeated. You are perfectly and wonderfully made to fit your purpose in life and to fulfil your mission in life. So, appreciate yourself and do not let anything put you down or make you feel inferior. "No one can make you feel inferior without your permission."[82]

Your Purpose

Your purpose relates to your assignment in life. It is about your vocation or calling in life. What is your assignment in life? How do you identify and fulfil it? This world does not belong to any one of us, it is a stage for each of us to perform our roles. Thus, we all own a part of it through our contribution. So be confident, what is important is what you bring to the table of humanity. Frankl observes, "Everyone has his own specific vocation or mission in life; everyone must carry out a concrete assignment that demands fulfilment. Therein, he cannot be replaced, nor can his life be repeated. Thus, everyone's task is unique, as is his specific opportunity to implement it."

When you know yourself and you understand why you exist, you can handle anything that may come your way. The world recognizes and rewards our contribution, not our mere looks or qualifications. With focus,

---

[82]   Quote by Eleanor Roosevelt

faith, hard work and discipline, you can use what fate puts on your plate or in your hands for what you have to give to the world.

Viktor Frankl again observed: "A man who becomes conscious of the responsibility he bears toward a human being who affectionately waits for him, or to an unfinished work, will never be able to throw away his life. He knows the 'why' for his existence and will be able to bear almost any how." Here, Frankl indicates clearly that meaning in life is pivoted on purpose, which is the why of our existence. Success is therefore a measure of the achievement of our purpose in life. Therefore, we cannot talk about success in life without starting from our purpose in life. My question is, what is your purpose in life? Have you identified it yet and do you have a plan to fulfil it, or have you already fulfilled much of it?

Purpose is not merely about your career, but more about your impact. There are many people who have jobs but have misplaced their purpose. What impact do you want to make in life?

Passion

What drives you? Do you have any burning desire or enthusiasm? ***Purpose without passion is like a flat tire, it cannot move.*** Passion is that which drives you and gives you the enthusiasm to pursue the goals you set to accomplish the purpose. What is it that weighs so much in your heart that makes your adrenalin rush through your body any time you think about it? What is it that gives you so much discomfort that you feel that it should be changed? What is it that you do with so much ease that brings joy to people and makes you feel fulfilled? What is it that many people tell you that you are good at? What is it that you want to give to humanity for humanity to remember you for? That one thing that runs through all these questions could be your passion. Once you identify your passion, craft your purpose around that passion.

Locate your purpose and passion to start your journey to success. Diane Matyas puts it this way: "Passion is the overwhelming feeling, the burning desire, the drive that ultimately creates change. It is the total belief in yourself and your abilities that nothing can stop you."[83] Jason Williams also adds, "No matter what you do or how hard you try, you will

---

[83] Quote by Diane Matyas, non- dated

never please everybody. There will always be someone who disapproves of you. However, if you believe in yourself and your strengths, and you have conviction in what you do, you will still be successful." That conviction is your passion.

Be inspired by the words of Winston Churchill, British Prime Minister of resilience, that "Success consists of going from failure to failure without loss of enthusiasm." Malcolm Forbes also adds, that "The key to success is not through achievement, but through enthusiasm. Locate your enthusiasm and you will find your passion; in there you will find your purpose. Finally, be you and yourself, and do not let the competition define you because your purpose and timing are different from that of the competition. Let your passion define your competition. Be your own competitor with your passion.

Place

Where have you been called to serve? Accra, Nungua, Kumasi, New York, London, Cape Town, Africa, UK, USA or the whole world. When your assignment is in Nungua, but you find yourself in New York, you are likely to fail, and vice versa. Look again around you and examine whether you are where your contribution is needed and valued most.

What is your Price?

Your price is your value (worth) not what you value. It is the value you place on yourself and your worth to others. The fact that you place a certain value on yourself does not mean others value you the same way. The fact that you value some things, does not mean you place a certain level of value on yourself. Personal worth or price relates to self-worth, self-esteem, self-confidence, and the value that your self-confidence and esteem produces. On the other hand, the value you place on yourself, will not be the value others place on you. I have heard many people ask questions like: who is that person? Where did (s)he come from? How beautiful is she? She does not even look that good, who does she think she is? What makes her attract such people, and how can she occupy that position? I am sorry you got it all wrong because it is not just about personality, it is your value, the price tag you choose to put on yourself. If you make yourself cheap, people may take you for granted. However, your value or price is not akin to arrogance. It is about understanding what you carry and what that is worth. It is about being confident in what you carry and your worth to others, irrespective of how you look, or where you come from, or your social background.

Principles

When you do not know what you are living for, any wind can blow you in any direction. What moral values inform your actions and inaction? What are your likes and dislikes? What do you consider as virtues or vices? What do you consider to be right or wrong? How does your judgement about right and wrong inform what you are likely to do, or what you will not do, no matter how you are forced to? Your Principles are your anchor. They hold you firmly rooted in the storms and strives of life.

Now that you have located your purpose and passion, you need to identify your values. Your values are formed by what you cherish and what you dislike, what you are likely to do and what you will not do, irrespective of external pressure, because you stand for that. Your values are your backbone for behaviour.

Mindtools puts it this way: "Your values are the things that you believe are important in the way you live and work. They (should) determine your priorities, and, deep down, they are probably the measures you use to tell if your life is turning out the way you want it to."[84]

To define your personal values, you need to discover what is truly important to you in life. Different people consider different things important.

- caring for others
- personal wealth
- service
- obeying the rules
- proving accountability

---

[84]   Mindtools, What Are Your Values? Deciding What's Most Important in Life. https://www.mindtools.com/pages/article/newTED_85.htm

- reputation
- contribution
- power

The list is long. A good way to start thinking about your values is to look back at your life and identify situations that made you quite uncomfortable, or made you feel very good and inwardly satisfied with fulfilment, peace and harmony, and really confident that you were making good choices. List them down or describe them.

Step 1: Identify the situations when you were happiest and most unhappy

Describe that situation and identify what actually made you feel happy
Describe a situation where you were unhappy about something connected to your career or social life

Step 2: Identify the times when you were most proud

Describe it using examples from your career and personal life
What other things influenced your feelings of pride?

Step 3: Identify situations when you were most fulfilled and satisfied

What need or desire was fulfilled?
Why did the experience give fulfilment?
What other factors contributed to your feelings of fulfilment?

Step 4: Establish your values by listing individual factors that accounted for your experiences of happiness, pride, and fulfilment, at most four.

Rank them in the order of priority

Performance

Performance relates to your execution power. Performance requires consistent action geared towards the achievement of results. Performance is more than effort. Action without results is wasted effort. It is often said that finishing is more important than starting. How you finish is more important than how you started. Between starting and finishing, there is always a gap. That gap is filled by action and response. Poor action will give you poor results no matter how good you think you are. Consistent outstanding actions will give you excellent results, not simply because the action is good, but because the actions are outstanding and consistent.

Contribution is important, but not at the Expense of Your Purpose and Values

Many of us believe that helping people is key to fulfilment in life. Yes, we live because of our purpose, which connects us to humanity. However, we need to understand the place and time of helping others in our mission in life. Helping others at the expense of personal purpose is stupidity. Recall the case of the light housekeeper who worked on a rocky coastline and received a monthly supply of oil to keep the light burning so that ships would not wreck. He gave his supplies to the village woman who begged for some oil to keep her family warm. Because the requests seemed legitimate, the lighthouse keeper tried to please people at the expense of his assignment and purpose. His oil was finished before his next supplies, causing several ships to wreck and the loss of several lives. The man had several excuses for why it happened, though he chose to please others at the expense of his purpose and duty. Obviously, he is likely to have lost his job. The lighthouse keeper lacked focus on his purpose. He substituted his purpose with the service of people he was not called to serve, a deviation from personal purpose – lack of focus. How many times have you pleased people at the expense of what is expected of you? Focus and discipline to the purpose is critical to success and the achievement of our goals in life.

Note that a person's purpose may reach far beyond that individual. It can affect families, communities, societies, and even unborn generations. You need to act with purpose and strong will. Do not trade your mission for satisfying others and living their purpose instead of focusing on your own. We need to be sensitive to obstructions to our main purpose when trying to respond to calls from others.

I once visited Tripoli, Libya, and some Ghanaian friends were exceedingly hospitable to me. They bought a new bed just so I could stay with them for two days and prepared a dinner in my honour. Before I left, the lady of the home (Efi) took me round the city to shop. Efi and I had been neighbours back home, but not close. In the process of shopping, I bought a number of clothes recommended by Efi. Though they were not my taste, I felt obliged to satisfy my pleasant hostess. As it turned out, I never used those clothes. Five years later I gave the clothes away. Those were not my clothes, they were Efi's clothes that I paid for because I wanted to make her happy. The choice of clothes did not define me, they define Efi. I learnt not to be unduly influenced against my wishes or principles. Do not live other people's purpose, dreams, values or principles. Understand who you are and what makes you unique. Stop living within the confines of how others define you. You were not created to live their lives, but yours. "Never dull your shine for somebody else." - Tyra Banks.

Know and Understand your Personality

Personality is the distinguishing patterns of thoughts, feelings, and behaviours that make a person unique. It is believed that personality arises from within the individual as they are born with traits that remains fairly consistent throughout life, although they can be influenced by an individual's family, culture, or their experiences. A person's personality plays a role in how they behave and interact with other people and within their world.[85] Personality has multiple expressions. It can be displayed in your behaviour or your thoughts, feelings, close relationships, and other social interactions. Shannon Alder observes that "personality begins, where comparison leaves off" because there is no basis for comparison as each of us have a unique personality, though there are some generic features which can be identified with a personality test. It is therefore important to be unique, confident and memorable (your brand and style should be memorable).

---

[85] Kylie Rymanowicz, Michigan State University Extension - October 18, 2017, The Nine Traits of Temperament, https://www.canr.msu.edu/news/the_nine_traits_of_temperament, Retrieved 18th June 2021

To understand your personality amounts to answering the question, who are you? Take a moment to reflect on yourself and describe who you are. Also reflect on your style. What is it that you can be remembered for in terms of your style? Style is a reflection of your appearance, attitude and your disposition.[86] A beautiful appearance will last a few decades, but a beautiful personality will last a lifetime. Edmond Mbiaka admonishes, "there is nothing more attractive than a great positive personality. Its beauty never fades away with time." It is believed that people's personality is defined by the way we come across to others in terms of how we appear, how we relate, our confidence, how we behave and even talk. Generally, the following types of personalities have been identified based on the different theories.

PERSONALITY TYPES, TRAITS / DIMENSIONS AND TEMPERAMENTS

There are different types of personality theories. Personality can be defined by type, traits, dimensions and temperaments. The "Big Five Forces, for example, classify personality by traits, while the Four Types of personality, the Meyers-Briggs Type Indicator (MBTI), and the Enneagram classify personality by type. There is also the proto–Psychological Personality which classifies personalities by Temperaments, like the Four Temperament by Galen based on the four humour model of Hippocrates,[87] and recently the Michigan State University (MSU) Temperament that uses nine traits to classify personality temperaments of individuals. It is important to note that there are still controversies regarding the different personality theories. What is described below are a few selected popular ones to guide an understanding of self.

---

[86]   - Shawn Ashmore,

[87]   Donnellan, M. Brent; Robins, Richard W. (2010). "Resilient, Overcontrolled, and Undercontrolled Personality Types: Issues and Controversies". *Social and Personality Psychology Compass.* **4** (11): 1070–1083. doi:10.1111/j.1751-9004.2010.00313.x. ISSN 1751-9004.

FOUR TYPES OF PERSONALITIES88

Type A: Perfectionist, impatient, competitive, work-obsessed, achievement-oriented, aggressive, stressed.

Type B: Low stress, even-tempered, flexible, creative, adaptable to change, patient, tendency to procrastinate.

Type C: Highly conscientious, perfectionist, struggles to reveal emotions (positive and negative)

Type D: feelings of worry, sadness, irritability, pessimistic outlook, negative self-talk, avoidance of social situations, lack of self-confidence, fear of rejection, appearing gloomy, hopelessness[89,90]

PERSONALITY TRAITS: THE BIG FIVE FORCES

Personality Trait theorists have tried to identify exactly how many personality traits exist. Some theories suggest a variety of possible traits, including Gordon Allport's list of 4,000 personality traits, Raymond Cattell's 16 personality factors, and Hans Eysenck's three-factor theory.[91]

Cattell's theory has been described as too complicated, while Eysenck's is considered too limited in scope. Consequently, the five-factor theory emerged to describe the essential traits considered the building blocks of personality. The Big Five Personality traits are believed to be core personality traits that feed both the Meyers-Briggs (MBTI) and the Enneagram.[92] The "big five" are broad categories of personality traits. These are *Openness, Conscientiousness, Extraversion or Extroversion, Agreeableness, and Neuroticism* (OCEAN).

---

[88] Find more on personality types at https://selfhelpforlife.com/four-main-personality-types/ https://www.hiresuccess.com/help/understanding-the-4-personality-types

[89] Very Well Mind, https://www.verywellmind.com/what-is-personality-2795416, retrieved 12th April, 2021.

[90] Very Well Mind, https://www.verywellmind.com/what-is-personality-2795416

[91] Kendra Cherry, The Big Five Forces, Retrieved by David Susman, 20th February, 2021 https://www.verywellmind.com/the-big-five-personality-dimensions-2795422, retrieved May 22, 2021

[92] What is the Difference between the Big five, MBTI and Enneagram https://www.retorio.com/blog/pre-employment-assessment-big-5?

Openness: Openness relates to imagination and insight. People with high openness are curious and keen to learn and experience new things making them quite adventurous. People low in this feature are often more traditional and conservative.

Openness

High	Low
Very creative	Dislikes change
Open to trying new things	Does not enjoy new things
Focused on tackling new challenges	Resists new ideas
Happy to think about abstract concepts	Not very imaginative
Likes Theoretical concepts	Dislikes abstract or theoretical concepts

Conscientiousness features thoughtfulness, good impulse control, and goal-directed behaviours. Highly conscientious people tend to be organized and mindful of details. They plan ahead, think about how their behaviour affects others, and are mindful of deadlines.

Conscientiousness

High	Low
Spends time preparing	Dislikes structure and schedules
Finishes important tasks right away	Makes messes and doesn't take care of things
Pays attention to detail	Fails to return things or put them back where they belong
Enjoys having a set schedule	Procrastinates important tasks
Completes tasks in a timely manner	Fails to complete necessary or assigned tasks

Extraversion

Extraversion is marked by high emotional expressions, excitability, sociability, talkativeness, and assertiveness. People high on this feature are outgoing and social. Being around other people helps them feel energized and excited. People low in extraversion are reserved and often require a period of solitude and quiet in order to "recharge."

High	Low
Enjoys being the centre of attention	Prefers solitude
Likes to start conversations	Feels exhausted when having to socialize a lot
Enjoys meeting new people	Finds it difficult to start conversations
Has a wide social circle of friends and acquaintances	Dislikes making small talk
Finds it easy to make new friends	Carefully thinks things through before speaking
Feels energized when around other people	Dislikes being the centre of attention
Says things before thinking about them	How Extroversion in Personality Influences Behaviour

Agreeableness

This feature relates to trust, altruism, kindness, affection, and other social oriented and citizenship behaviours. High agreeableness tends to be more cooperative while low agreeableness tend to be more competitive and sometimes even manipulative.

High	Low
Feels empathy and concern for other people	Takes little interest in others
Cares about others	Doesn't care about how other people feel

Has a great deal of interest in other people	Has little interest in other people's problems
Enjoys helping and contributing to the happiness of other people	Insults and belittles others
Assists others who are in need of help	Manipulates others to get what they want

Neuroticism

Neuroticism is characterized by sadness, moodiness, and emotional instability. Individuals who are high in this trait tend to experience mood swings, anxiety, irritability, and sadness. Those low in this trait tend to be more stable and emotionally resilient.

Tablexx: Neuroticsm

High	Low
Experiences a lot of stress	Emotionally stable
Worries about many different things	Deals well with stress
Gets upset easily	Rarely feels sad or depressed
Experiences dramatic shifts in mood	Doesn't worry much
Feels anxious	Is very relaxed
Struggles to bounce back after stressful events	Adaptable and deals with stress in a collected manner

Temperaments

Temperament are traits that define how people react to the world. Are you quiet or noisy? Irritable or stable? Adaptable or conservative? The temperament is mostly innate and inborn traits, although they can be influenced by an individual's environment (family, culture or their experiences). There are two sets of temperaments identified in this book. These are the Four Old Temperament theory by Galen based on the four humour model of Hippocrates and the MSU nine traits of temperament theory which is more current.

THE FOUR TYPES OF TEMPERAMENT93

The Four temperaments is a proto-psychological theory that suggests that there are four fundamental personality types, sanguine (enthusiastic, active, and social), choleric (short-tempered, or irritable), melancholic (analytical, wise, and quiet), and phlegmatic (relaxed and peaceful).[94] Take a temperament test at https://psychologia.co/four-temperaments-test/

The MSU Temperaments[95]

In recent times, the Michigan State University (MSU) has described nine traits of temperament which define how someone reacts to the world. These include Activity Level, Biological Rhythm, Sensitivity, Intensity of reaction, Adaptability, Approach and withdrawal, Persistence, Distractibility, and Mood.

Adaptability

Adaptability means how easily someone can adjust to change or new situations. Highly adaptable people can easily switch from one activity or location to another, without any problems. Those who are less adaptable need to take time to feel comfortable with change or new situations.

Activity level

Activity level refers to how physically active a person is. Some people feel the need to be up and moving and on the go all the time, whereas other people are more likely to move more slowly and engage in quieter, calmer activities.

---

[93] https://www.betterhelp.com/advice/temperament/4-most-common-temperament-types/ Retrieved 3rd May, 2020

[94] https://psychologia.co/four-temperaments-test/, Retrieved 3rd May 2021

[95] Kylie Rymanowicz, The nine traits of temperament, Michigan State University Extension - October 18, 2017, https://www.canr.msu.edu/news/the_nine_traits_of_temperament, retrieved 7th May.

Biological Rhythm

Biological rhythms relate to the consistency of internal drives, like eating, sleeping and bathing. Some individuals do have very consistent routines; for example, they wake up at the same time each day, eat around the same time, and sleep at the same time. Others may be more inconsistent and find it difficult to stick to rigid routines.

Sensitivity

People high on sensitivity react more strongly to sound, light, touch, smell and taste. They may be troubled by bright lights and loud noises. Their reactions to these stimuli could be intense; what appears like a small nuisance could trigger a big response.

Intensity of reaction

People react very differently to situations. Some people react very mildly while others react more strongly to both positive and negative situations. People with lower intensity may only smile when they receive good news, whereas others who react more intensely may jump up and down and run around at the same good news.

Approach and withdrawal

Approach and withdrawal refer to how quickly and easily a person adjusts to changes or new situations and people. Some people may find it easy to adapt to new situations while others require more time to warm up to new situations and people.

Persistence

Persistence refers to the ability and willingness to stick to a task, even when it is challenging. Some people can hold on to something, even when they run into roadblocks along the way. Other people may be more willing to drop a task that is difficult and move on to something else.

Distractibility

Distractibility simply refers to how easily someone is distracted by their environment. People who get distracted easily may have their attention pulled from the task at hand by ambient noise or other people or things in the background. Those who are not easily distracted will find it easy to be absorbed in a task despite outside stimuli.

Mood

Mood refers to the overall tone of a person's feelings, interactions and behaviours. Some people are dispositioned to have a happier overall mood, and they generally feel good about things. Others may have more of a negative mood. They may be referred to as more unpleasant, as they may not react in a strong, positive way with the world around them.

THE MYERS-BRIGGS TYPE INDICATOR (MBTI)

The Myers Briggs Type Indicator has 4 dimensions that reveals how an individual gathers information and makes decisions. The 4 dimensions provide 16 different combinations, which create 16 different types of personalities. The four pairs of dimensions are extroversion/introversion, Sensing /Intuition, Thinking/Feeling, and Judging/Perceiving. To know what your personality is you can take a test at https://www.16personalities.com/free-personality-test.

THE ENNEAGRAM

The Enneagram has nine main, overarching types that interact with each other in unique ways. It's common for a person to exhibit more than one trait of Enneagram type. The nine are "Mediator, Perfectionist, Advisor, Achiever, individualist, Thinker, Guardian, Optimist, Challenger. You can take an Enneagram type Test at https://www.truity.com/test/enneagram-personality-test

KNOW WHAT WORKS FOR YOUR PHYSICAL BODY

Foods

We need to be alive and healthy to fulfil our goals and be successful. When you are sick, your goals and dreams will suffer, and when you die, your goals come to an end. So, you need to be alive and well to pursue your purpose and passion. Wellbeing has been defined as 'a positive physical, social and mental state'.

What you eat, how you eat** and **the time you eat are important aspects of our wellbeing. Food and water are the building blocks of the physical body.[96] Our health, energy levels and mood depend on the foods we eat. However, not all foods work the same way for everybody. It is said that one man's meat is another man's poison. For example, I used to feel very sick and weak frequently. At a point, it was always embarrassing for me to complain about my health. It took one doctor to advise that I start recording what I eat on a daily basis and observe how I feel. Through this, I observed a number of foods that make me feel sick and realised I was allergic to a number of foods recommended as healthy.

Knowing what foods we should and shouldn't be eating can be very helpful for our wellbeing. There is enough evidence which suggests that in addition to affecting our physical health, what we eat may also affect the way we feel. Make sure your food is balanced with fruits and vegetables, protein, and grains that work for you. Stay hydrated with at least 1.5 litres of water a day. It's recommended that you drink between 6–8 glasses of fluid a day, these may include tea, coffee, smoothies, among others, but be careful of sugar and caffeine. Water is therefore a good option for hydration.

Knowing what foods work for you and improving your diet and water intake can help you feel better, so you can achieve your goals and aspirations.

---

[96]   Department of Health (2010). ***Healthy Lives, Healthy People: Our strategy for public health in England***. London: The Stationery Office. Available at: https://www.gov.uk/government/uploads/system/uploads/attachment_data/file/216096/dh_127424.pdf [Accessed on 04/11/15]. Retrieved 20th March, 2021

Though many people have all sorts of conspiracy theories about blood type eating, I noted that many of the foods I had observed from my personal notes that were not good for me, were also part of the foods listed in my blood type eating by Dr Peter J D'Adamo as foods that were not good for my blood type. Though not all the recommendations by D'Amato worked for me, the majority (80-90%) of them worked for me or did not work for me just as his theory put forward. It may or may not work for you, but it is worth reading about it since they seem to have some benefits. Should you be interested in blood type eating, you can follow the link https://www.webmd.com/diet/a-z/blood-type-diet, or https://www.medicalnewstoday.com/articles/319399#foods-recommended-by-the-diet.

How We Eat: Eating regularly and the Portions we eat

Apart from what works for you, how you eat is also important. The portions and timing of what we eat goes a long way to affect our wellbeing. Eating at irregular times and starving yourself and then binging on heavy meals have been proven to be unhealthy. How often you eat, and the portions are important too, as they affect blood sugar levels. Blood sugar controls our energy levels and general well-being. When our blood sugar drops, we might feel tired, irritable and depressed, the same as when our blood sugar goes up. Eating regularly and choosing foods that release energy slowly will help to keep your sugar levels steady. Grains like oats, rice, millet, cereals, nuts and seeds are slow energy release foods.[97]

Late night eating

Eating late at night has been proven to be associated with several health hazards like indigestion, acid reflux, increase in blood sugar levels, heart diseases, and obesity. Essentially, the later or closer to bedtime you eat, the less your body is prepared to sleep, which can also have adverse effects on your memory and efficiency for the next day. I noticed that one critical factor in keeping my stomach from bulging was how late I eat my last meal.

---

[97]   Food and Mood, December 2017, https://www.mind.org.uk/information-support/tips-for-everyday-living/food-and-mood/about-food-and-mood/ Retrieved 20th March, 2021

When I eat at the latest by 5 or 7pm for a week, my stomach and waistline drops significantly, though the portion I eat is equally important.[98]

Exercise

Physical activity has been proven to be good for the physical body. Having a healthy heart, joints, and regular bowel movements, are some of the benefits of exercise. Physical activity is also beneficial for mental health and wellbeing. However, people generally have different stress tolerance levels, and this is very important to consider when choosing physical exercises. As little as short bursts of 10 minutes' brisk walking can increase our mental alertness, energy, positive mood and can reduce stress and anxiety.[99] I normally felt sick whenever I exercised vigorously until I took a stress test and realized that my body and heart are not made for strenuous exercises, so I resorted to walking at least 30 minutes a day, sometimes in my room, and that has worked quite well for me. Though in my fifties, many often assume I am about twenty years younger.

Wellbeing through mindfulness

Mindfulness is a means by which we pay attention to the present moment and our being through techniques like meditation, breathing, yoga, and listening to calm music. It helps us become more aware of our thoughts and feelings so that we can manage them. Mindfulness can therefore be employed to manage your wellbeing and mental or emotional health.[100] There are times when we feel a little down, stressed or frightened. Most of the time we are able to deal with such feeling and they just go away, but sometimes they develop into more serious problems and this

---

[98] Does Eating Late At Night Cause Weight Gain? Health Hazards Of Eating Late At Night. https://www.ndtv.com/health/does-eating-late-at-night-cause-weight-gain-other-health-hazards-of-eating-late-at-night-1925980

[99] How to look after our Mental health Using Exercise, 2021, https://www.mentalhealth.org.uk/publications/how-to-using-exerciseHow Retrieved 20th March 2021.

[100] Baer, R.A. (2003). Mindfulness Techniques as a Clinical Intervention: A Conceptual and Empirical Review. Clinical Psychology Science and Practice, 10 (2), 125–143.

could happen to any one of us. Managing your mental health is important because good mental health, can help you make the most of your potential - because our thoughts control our actions. The benefit of mindfulness to health and wellbeing is well established though the knowledge is still growing. This includes the mind, the brain, the body, and behaviour.[101] A person's relationships with others and addictive behaviours such as alcohol or substance misuse and gambling, also affect our mental health.[102] Being alone sometimes, being quiet and listening to your body and mind is important. Locate what works for you and practice it.

Grooming

Grooming refers to the things that people do to keep themselves clean and make their face, hair, skin and nails look nice. Men and women's grooming habits are one of the first things that others will notice. This includes body care, facials, pedicure, manicure, perfume, a well-kept beard among others. Furthermore, keeping yourself well-presented kindles your own self-esteem and offer more confidence and a self-assured impression. This is not to say you should dedicate all your effort to working on your body or try and emulate fashion icons on social media, TV, or in magazines. You just have to be well-kept and presentable. The unique appearance and image you put forth communicates volumes about your personality.

Clothing and Appearance

In addition to feeling good about yourself through proper grooming, eating right, and mindfulness, we also need to choose the right clothing that suits the occasion and our bodies. Our appearance and the clothes we wear tells a lot about us, and the initial impressions of a person are often

---

[101] Greeson, J.M. (2008). Mindfulness research update: 2008. **Complementary Health Practice Review 14,** 10–8..

[102] Carson, J.W., Carson, K.M., Gil, K.M. & Baucom, D.H. (2004). Mindfulness-based relationship enhancement. **Behavior Therapy. 35**, 471–494.
How to look after Your Mental H alth Using Mindfulness, 2021, https://www.mentalhealth.org.uk/publications/how-look-after-your-mental-health-using-mindfulness, Retrieved 20th March, 2021

based on the image he or she portrays. People judge you based on how you portray yourself externally. Looking your best is a great way to boost your self-esteem. There is nothing as satisfying as looking at yourself in the mirror in the morning and feeling genuinely satisfied. Some people may think that buying expensive clothes or designer wear, driving the most striking car, living in a plush house, or a high-powered job is all that they need to display a quality image.

Appearance is, however, very essential. People judge your outward appearance before they experience what you have to offer. You must establish your own signature appearance or style, one that brands you, identifies you, and attracts respect and favour to your personality. Your character may not be exposed at a first encounter, but your appearance will. Whether right or not, we are an image-driven society and many of the first impressions that we make are based on what our eyes see. Focus on your appearance, it is part of how you get the relationships and respect that can make you successful.

In managing your appearance, it is important to know what suits your body type, shape and face so that you can choose clothing that enhance your features and make the right statements. Often, we tend to follow fashion or the crowd and go for clothes that portray us negatively or hairstyles that do not suit our face shape. There are about seven different face shapes, namely; rectangle or oblong, oval, square, round, triangle, heart and diamond.

The following describes face shapes and general styles[103]

Rectangle/ Oblong: Sharp jaw, and broad forehead, similar width, generally elongated face. People with Oblong face shape should soften their appearance without further elongating the face. Layered cuts, waves or curls, or rounded fringes work.

Oval: Well-balanced appearance, Blunt bobs and lobs with subtle layers, long waves or curls are often suitable.

Square: Face features a broad forehead, wide cheekbones, and a strong jawline. Style should be side-parted styles, long and airy layers, short layered bobs, side-swept bangs

---

[103]   https://www.thetrendspotter.net/haircuts-for-face-shape/ Retrieved 21st May 2021

Heart: Bone structure will feature a broad forehead and cheekbones with a narrow jawline and chin. Style should be long side-swept cuts, waves or curls starting below the ear, side-parted pixies, bobs and lobs

Diamond: Diamond is an angular face shape that features a narrow forehead and jawline with cheekbones at the widest point of the face. Mid or long layered cuts worn with tousled waves, deep side parts, chin-length bobs, ponytails at the back of the head.

Round: Similar length and width as well as prominent, rounded cheeks. Long layered cuts, choppy pixie cuts, short side bangs

Triangle: Strong jawline that is wider than the forehead and a chin that is square or flat in shape. Style should be layers that finish at the eyes/cheekbones or collarbone, choppy pixie cuts, short side bangs. To identify your face shape and the recommended hairstyles visit https://www.thetrendspotter.net/haircuts-for-face-shape/.

Dressing

Dressing is a key part of appearance, but different from simply clothing. Two people may have the same clothes but dress differently. Dressing is how we combine clothes, hair make up, bags, belt, and shoes to make a complete appearance statement. It is also important to know how to dress for every occasion and environment. Modesty is golden and there is beauty and honour in simplicity. Most importantly, you need to create a signature style and brand for your personality. It is also important to apprise yourself of dress etiquette. For example, for men, what type of shirt goes with what type of trouser or shoes, or necktie and belt? For women, what type of fabric and style will suit a particular occasion, and how should your make-up be worn? Once again, make up is an important part of a lady's appearance. Make up should generally be subtle, with the undertones and blusher understated. For dress etiquette please visit https://brightside.me/inspiration-tips-and-tricks/14-dressing-rules-that-everyone-should-learn-once-and-for-all-441210/ or https://www.managementstudyguide.com/clothing-etiquettes.htm..

Like anything in life, building a brand or image, impressing others, building strong relationships where individuals respect you for who you are, takes time, dedication, commitment, and should go much deeper than simply the designer jeans you bought or the car you drive.

CHAPTER 11

HUMAN CAPITAL: WHAT DO YOU KNOW, AND WHAT ARE YOU DOING WITH IT?

*This Chapter is dedicated to Naomi Borley Alabi,
my daughter, for her contributions*

THE CONCEPT OF HUMAN CAPITAL

In the 21st Century we need wisdom, not mere knowledge to succeed. Human Capital is an expression of your wisdom. Human Capital is your "know-how and know-what; and what you do with your know how and know what". If you have knowledge that is not producing value beyond you, it is not a human capital. Your human capital refers to the skills, competencies, qualifications, abilities, attitude, and execution power you have. Your human capital is required to achieve your personal goals. Your human capital is a combination of your skills, competences, abilities, and attitudes. Knowledge can be acquired through schooling, reading or experience. Skills and abilities, on the other hand, can be acquired through training and practice. Not all of your human capital is acquired in school or the classroom. Attitude develops mostly outside class. The dictionary describes attitude as a settled way of thinking or feeling about something. It often defines our response or reactions to situations, in other words, attitudes are developed through personal values and resolve. In psychology, an attitude refers to a set of emotions, beliefs, and behaviours

114

toward a particular object, person, thing, or event. Therefore, attitude is mostly informed by our values. Attitudes are often the result of experience, upbringing, or nurturing, and they can have a powerful influence over behaviour. While attitudes are enduring, they can also change." [104]

Going forward in the 21st Century, traditional qualifications may at best open some doors for us. More and more, it is becoming evident that the world of work is shifting more towards skill, abilities and attitude (the soft skills) than qualifications. It is therefore essential to consider acquiring soft skills and abilities (technical skills) suitable for the 21st Century. These include *Learning skills* (the ability to unlearn and learn new things, to accept criticisms and take what is good from them, to re-enforce a good habit, or to do away with habits that are less desirable). It also includes Thinking, Creativity, Communication and Collaboration; *Literacy skills* (Technology, media and current information); and *Life Skills* (Problem-solving, Collaboration and Team skills, Leadership, flexibility, social-skills, initiative and productivity skills, time management skills). Hard or technical skills like artificial intelligence, robotics, machine learning, nanotechnology, beauty and fashion, biological research, health, teaching, waste management, organic food chain, food science, nutrition, renewable energy, energy technicians, logistics, telecommunication, social media publishing, journalism, transportation, piloting, fashion, law, engineering, agribusiness, accounting, and auditing, are some of the professional skills that may suffice in the 21st Century, though the list is not exhaustive. What Skills, Competences and Abilities do you need to achieve your personal vision? Take some time to reflect and list them.

In the book of Proverbs, it is written, "Wisdom is the principal thing; therefore, get wisdom, and in all thy getting, get understanding (Proverbs 4:7, NKJV). Wisdom for me is the application of knowledge plus an awareness of the limitations of what we know at any given time, and what we do not know. This means wisdom comes with knowledge. Being aware of the limitations of what you know and what you do not know should make you a learning person, not the learned. Remember, Eric Hoffer observed: "in times of change, learners inherit the earth; while the learned

---

[104] https://www.google.com/search?q=attitude+definition+psychology&client=safari&channel=iphone_bm&sxsrf=ALeKk00UxmiVZ- Retrieved 18th March, 2021

find themselves beautifully equipped to deal with a world that no longer exists." [105]

TALENT, SKILLS AND ABILITIES

Many of us confuse our gifts and talents with our abilities. Talents are natural gifts and the capacity to do something effortlessly. Skill on the other hand is an acquired ability, learned with effort. Ability is possession of skill to do something. Serena and Venessa Williams may have had talents and gifts for playing Tennis, but their talents did not make them world champions, their skills and abilities did. Like Pablo Escobar the Champion Criminal, Venessa and Serena Williams had to train relentlessly to acquire the skills needed to win championships. They continued to hone their skills with utmost dedication and discipline. They had the attitude of champions, a winning mindset, and their abilities made them world champions. They had skill and style on the pitch. They were competent in the knowledge of tennis and had the attitude of winners. They had a practical doctorate degree in playing tennis. They trained to be champions, psyched themselves to be champions, and they became champions. Their success came not only, from their passion and purpose to play, but from training and psychological resolve (their attitude). Without training, education, knowledge, skills and the right attitude, our human capital will not be adequate to support our success on the journey of life, or at best produce ambiguous outcomes.

Some of us also have all the knowledge and information but are not using it to our advantage. It is important to examine at this point what you're doing with your knowledge and abilities? That is your execution power.

Execution Power

Remember we started with wisdom, and we said it is the application of what you know? Knowledge which is not put to use is useless and will not help you achieve your dreams. Whatever your vision, purpose and

---

105

passion, what is important is not your wish list or your dream, but how you are executing your plan. A journey of a thousand miles begins with a step. Then step after step, you arrive at your destination. So come on, make that important step and start implementing that plan.

Execution, Planning, Discipline and Problem Solving

Discipline and Consistency

"Victory awaits they that have everything in order - Luck people call it. Defeat is certain for him who has neglected to take the necessary precautions in time: this is called bad luck". Roald Amunsden – The South Pole.

Authors Jim Collins and Morten T. Hansen, along with a team of 20 researchers, set out to answer the question: Why do some companies thrive in uncertainty, even chaos, and others do not? The group analysed seven companies that performed not just better than their industry, but ten times better, and reported the findings in their book "*Great by Choice*". They discovered a very interesting key finding. The qualities that business gurus frequently projected as being the main difference-makers are things like innovation, creativity, and the ability to quickly adapt in a fast-changing world – were indeed somewhat important, but it was actually *discipline – fanatic discipline,* the discipline that comes with focusing on a particular goal and working towards it **consistently,** no matter what comes your way. The second is what they called *empirical creativity* (Problem Solving), that is learning from available evidence and facts to chart your own path without necessarily re-inventing the wheel. Thirdly, is what they called *productive paranoid*, that is, being positive while cognisant of risks associated with your confidence and how to navigate them. These are the true master keys of the companies' and their individual leaders' success, they reported.[106]

As Collins and Hansen explain in the book that emerged from their research on great companies, these companies that became Great by Choice did it through *careful, consistent discipline.* Collins and Morten

---

106

dubbed the slow and steady approach taken by great companies, *The 20-Mile March*, most probably derived from the Scott and Amundsen Race to the South Pole. Collins and Morten imagined a man determined to walk across the United States, and how he could accomplish his goal faster by committing to walking 20 miles every single day – rain or shine – rather than walking for 40-50 miles in good weather, and then very few miles or not at all during inclement conditions. Collins and Hansen recalled and related their theory of fanatic discipline, empirical creativity, and productive paranoid to the case of the epic contest between Falcon Scott and Amundsen in their race to the South Pole.

Instead of constantly changing course, or making really aggressive moves and taking big risks, "the great companies came up with a goal, a plan, and carefully, methodically, and consistently stuck with that plan; they move towards their long-term goals instead of getting side-tracked by short-term temptations, fears, and changing circumstances. They didn't panic during stormy periods, nor did they expand too aggressively during good times. Moderation and focus are golden rules of success.

Discipline and consistency are key elements of your execution power and human capital. Productivity and excellence is mostly achieved through discipline and consistency. Execution without discipline and consistency produces ad hoc and ambiguous results. In the book *Great by Choice*, Jim Collins pitches the 20-Mile Rule for the pursuit of great success, a principle for discipline and consistency developed from the epic race to the South Pole in 1911. Jim Collins adds that the 20-mile rule was developed from rigorous research of successful companies and their leaders, and discipline was recognised as a distinguishing factor that separates great organizations and leaders from good ones.[107]

THE RACE TO THE SOUTH POLE AND THE 20-MILE RULE

In 1910, two explorers began their quests to become the first men to ever set foot upon the southernmost point on earth. It was the "Heroic Age of Antarctic Exploration", and the South Pole represented one of the

---

[107]   Jim Collins, Twenty Mile Rule, 2021, https://www.jimcollins.com/concepts/twenty-mile-march.html, retrieved 12th April, 2021

last unexplored areas on earth. Robert Falcon Scott hoped to claim the bottom of the world for England; Roald Amundsen wished to plant the Norwegian flag there on behalf of his countrymen.

Despite their common goal, the two adventurers' approaches to their expeditions were quite different – as were the end results. Amundsen reached the South Pole first and returned home on a trip that was relatively smooth and straightforward. Scott arrived at 90 Degrees South 33 days later, only to experience the crushing disappointment of seeing one of Amundsen's flags flapping in the wind. He never made it back; he and his four companions died of starvation, exhaustion, and exposure as they attempted to make the 700-mile return trip to their base camp.

Amundsen's team left for the Pole with over 50 dogs on the 20th of October 1911. Amundsen had studied the Eskimos and saw that they used dogs to journey across the snow. Amundsen's strategy was simple. The dogs will do most of the work in transporting their equipment, while the men travel *fifteen to twenty miles a day* (*the 20 miles march*) in a six-hour period each day. This will allow both the dogs and men to have enough time to rest. Amundsen planned the journey very carefully, taking into consideration the risks and failures that were likely to occur and putting in measures to pre-empt them. Amundsen's team stocked their supply depot all along the route and had more depots than Scott.

The British party also arrived in Antarctica in January 1911. Scott chose to set up his base camp at McMurdo Sound. As Scott's men laid more depots, individual support teams and dogs successively turned back.

On the 1st of November, 1911, Scott left base camp with support parties, motor sledges, dogs, and ponies for his journey south. Scott's team planned to use motorised sledges, which could be aided by ponies and men should the necessity arise. As should be expected for such demanding trips, Scott's motor sledges broke down and stopped working five days into the trip. The ponies suffered in the extreme cold and were ultimately sacrificed for food. Scott did not learn from the Eskimos, he tried to reinvent the wheel rather than improve on it (Empirical Creativity). The team members had to drag the two-hundred-pound sledges. The Team did not stick to a pre-arranged, targeted distance to accomplish each day, instead they walked for long distances on good days with good weather, and short distances on days that were not so favourable. They worked with boosts of energy rather than planned moderate energy. The team's clothes, boots and googles were also affected by the harsh weather, and as a result, they developed serious frostbite which made it very difficult for them to continue with the journey without interruptions. Each day several hours were spent getting boots on the infected frostbitten feet of the men. The men also became snow-blind as a result of the unanticipated uncertainties. The team was also low on food and water. The paraffin used for heating and cooking had evaporated because the canisters containing the paraffin were so poorly made.

On the 17th of January, 1912, Scott arrived at the Pole - 33 days after Amundsen, to see the Norwegian victory signalled by the Norwegians' flag flapping in the wind. They had already embarked upon their return voyage, but he had left a tent containing surplus equipment. Amundsen had even left Scott a note to deliver to the King of Norway in case he did not return. The dispirited men took pictures and left quickly. Scott wrote gloomily in his diary: "The POLE. Yes, but under very different circumstances from those expected. Great God! This is an awful place and terrible enough for us to have laboured to it without the reward of priority. We will die like gentlemen." At this point all of Scott's men were suffering from slow starvation, hypothermia, and almost certainly scurvy. Petty Officer Evans was the first man to die on the 17th of February. A month later, on the 17th of March, Captain Oates, crippled with frostbite, walked out of the party's tent; it was his 32nd birthday – and his last day. A few days later, the three remaining men were lying in their tent waiting for death. Scott was the only one keeping his diary: "We shall stick it out to the end, but we are getting weaker, of course, and the end cannot be far. It seems a pity, but I do not think I can write more - R Scott."[108] The race to the Pole was over. All of Scott's men, and he himself, perished in the cold. ***Proper Planning and Preparation, Discipline and Consistency, Learning from Existing Evidence and Problem-Solving were established as keys to success.*** The race to the South Pole also establishes the 20-Mile Rule.

---

[108]   The Race to the South Pole, www.artofmanliness.com. Retrieved 15th April, 2021

CHAPTER 12

SOCIAL CAPITAL: YOUR SOCIAL INTELLIGENCE

Choose people who lift you up. - Michelle Obama

THE CONCEPT OF SOCIAL CAPITAL

Your qualification cannot always talk for you. The Oxford Dictionary defines Social Capital as the networks of relationships among people who live and work in a particular society, enabling that society to function effectively. So, your social capital refers to your network of people or people in your circles who enable you to achieve your purpose and passion in life; and make life meaningful for you. This includes your family, friends, people you work with or go/went to school with, associations you belong to, or church or religious members with whom you relate. However, not everyone in your environment is supposed to be in your circles. You choose who should be in your circles for a purpose. Your Social Capital is your connections that help you to achieve things that your qualifications and abilities are limited in efficacy.

There are three types of social capital: ***bonding social capital, bridging social capital and linking social capital.*** Bonding social capital refers to the links between like-minded (homogenous) people or ties between people in similar situations. It can be your neighbours, friends, or even family. "Bridging social capital can be referred to as the building of connections between unrelated groups, which are likely to be more fragile, but more likely also to foster social inclusion. Bridging social capital covers distant ties of like-minded persons, such as workmates and fast friends. Linking social capital, has to do with reaching out to people in unrelated situations, such as those who are entirely outside of the community, thus enabling members to leverage a far wider range of resources than are available in the community.[109] This will include your connections abroad, or in different circles from work, family, school etc. This may include connections on LinkedIn, Facebook, Snapchat or other social media. It will also include higher or lower circles that you may want to associate with for diversity. The whole idea of social capital is about social relationships. Its major elements include social networks, civic engagement, norms of reciprocity, and generalized trust. Always ask yourself what this relationship stands to offer me when deciding who to include in your network. Broadly speaking, Social Capital is defined as a collective asset in the form of shared norms, values, beliefs, networks, social relations, and institutions that facilitate cooperation and collective action for mutual benefit,[110] As capital, social capital is wealth, and an investment which should yield dividends or returns. Tim Sanders, said "Your network is your net worth." To what extent is your network influencing your net worth? It is time to assess your social capital and adjust it to suit you purpose and mission in life.

WHO IS IN YOUR CIRCLE OF FRIENDS?

There are many things that our qualifications, skills and abilities cannot do for us, but good relationships can. Some call it your connections. The people around you define how far you can go. Our friends, family and the surrounding people, influence our lives, health and wealth to a large extent. Often, we think that self-control comes from within, however,

---

[109] UKEssays. (November 2018). Definition and Types Of Social Capital. Retrieved from https://www.ukessays.com/essays/sociology/definition-and-types-of-social-capital-sociology-essay.php?vref=1Woolcock 2001: 13-4, Retrieved 15th April, 2021

[110] Humnath Bhandari and Kumi Yasunobu, What is Social Capital? A Comprehensive Review of the Concept, Asian Journal of Social Science, Volume 37, Number 3, 2009, pp. 480-510 https://www.researchgate.net/publication/233546004_What_Is_Social_Capital_A_Comprehensive_Review_of_the_Concept, retrieved 15th April, 2021.

many of our actions depend just as much on advice from our friends and family as ourselves. Those we surround ourselves with have the power to make us fit or unfit, drink more alcohol or no alcohol, smoke or do drugs, commit fraud or work with integrity, care more or less about the environment, work hard to be confident or have high self-esteem, or rob us of our self-confidence and esteem. Some people push us up while others bring us down. To succeed we need to consciously choose the people we want around us to achieve our goals and aspirations. Not everyone who wants to be in your circle should be there. We need to be selective about whom we align with, because our alliances can make or break us. A friend once told me that his father advised him to "walk with winners – period" and that is (www.). At first it sounded funny and a little too vain for me, but soon it started ringing in my mind www. "walk with winners" period and I started to appreciate the wisdom in that statement. What his father meant as he explained, was that when you walk in the company of winners, you could become a winner. Now I ask you, how many winners do you have in your network and what kind of winners are they? Can they contribute to your success? Are they people you met by chance or people you consciously sought to have in your network? Do they also feel obligated to do something for you whenever you call on them in the spirit of reciprocity? Those who do are part of your social capital, those who do not may be your social liabilities. Those who are part of your social capital are the people you can call when the need arises, and they will be there for you. When you surround yourself with successful people, you will be exposed to inspiring success stories that can help you cultivate your strive for success and excellence.

The blogger Simon Alexander Ong wrote "our success in life more often than not comes down to the people we choose to spend our time with. How smart you are, how talented you are., where you were born, the family environment you grew up in. All these may play some role as to how successful you will be in life, but in comparison to the impact of surrounding yourself with people who can lift you higher, they don't compare.

An individual maybe born into riches but live an unhappy life because he /she hooks up with junkies, whose lives are a waste and drug dependent, while someone from more humble beginnings maybe able to manifest their dreams in record-breaking time, all because of the company they keep, which influences their way of thinking and thus results in a mindset for success."[111] In a sentence, Michele Obama, former First Lady of the United States of America, summarizes it all "Choose people who lift you up".

It is key to note that being around positive minded individuals, who are focused and have a habit of chasing their dreams and believe in taking responsibility for their lives, propels you to grow in a positive direction as well. The people around you certainly have an impact on your thinking and consequently your behaviour. Choose those who are willing to support you on your journey and move you towards inspired action and productivity. Spend more time with your social capital rather than those who bring you down. When you are the best in your circle, who do you learn from? Choose to surround yourself with more of those who are ahead of you.

Robin Sharma, author of The *Monk Who Sold His Ferrari and the Leader Who Had No Tilte*, is quoted to observe: "Associate only with positive, focused people who you can learn from and who will not drain your valuable energy with uninspiring attitudes. By developing relationships with those committed to constant improvement and the pursuit of the best that life has to offer, you will have plenty of company on your path to the top of whatever mountain you seek to climb."

Fortunately, technology makes it simple for us to literally surround ourselves with inspiring people. From LinkedIn to Twitter, Facebook, Instagram and Snapchat – we can find the right people. At this point, I invite you to examine those around you and decide who ought to remain and who should not be in your new circle of friends and associates. Most importantly, be deliberate about who you choose to be in your social network.

You can begin creating a more optimal environment for your personal growth and success:

These days, you can build social capital through:

- Being very purposeful about the calibre of people you want to associate with

---

[111] Simon Alexander Ong, October 2013, How Your Circle of Friends influence who You Become https://www.simonalexanderong.com/2013/10/how-your-circle-of-friends-influence-who-you-become/, Retrieved 18th March, 2021

- Social Media Networks particularly LinkedIn, Twitter, Facebook, Instagram, Snapchat
- Attending physical events in your local town or city, even national or international events, conferences and online events like webinars that relate to your interests and purpose. Ensure that you have your business cards to network. Seek out people who have skills/qualities that you admire and can learn from them. Never assume that they have nothing to learn from you. You can always learn something from someone, regardless of where they are in their own life.
- Minimizing the time you spend hanging out with the wrong crowd and unhealthy influences, e.g. pessimists and those that can hurt your feelings on purpose or chances of achieving success.
- Reading more about the people you admire, and watching documentaries on Netflix, BBC and CNN etc. You will be exposed to inspiring success stories, expand your library of knowledge and nurture your creative thinking.
- Listening to audiobooks/podcasts when you are commuting and/or relaxing.
- Following inspirational people and those who you can learn from on social media channels and reach out for him.
- Subscribing to newsletters, which will add value to your life and help you towards your goals in life.
- Having an outlook of what you clearly want and remembering that, although it is important to spend your time with those who are more successful than you, it is also great for your development to be around those who are at the same stage as you in order to share ideas on how to move forward, and find ways to share your wisdom with those below you to serve as an inspiration.
- By all means spend less time in front of the TV and your smartphone, and more time getting out there and connecting with people. You just never know what it might lead to.

Your Thinking and How Your Social Circles Cap Your Thoughts

John C Maxwell, Bestselling author, describes in his book *Thinking for a Change* how a bull rider who wanted to move from the amateur club to the professional club discovered the importance of "thinking" his way to success during his career as a bull rider. According to Maxwell, during one of his conferences, a man approached him and told him about how he transitioned for the amateur bull-riding circuit to the league of world champions. He later wrote to him explaining the details of how our associations cap or limit our thinking, and what we can achieve. According to a letter I found on Maxwell's website, Richard McHugh indicated that he started bull riding with the amateur bull-riding circuit. He shortly moved to the top of the amateur circuit but yearned to join the professional bull riding association, so he looked to the top for a teacher. He met and started a relationship with a world champion bull rider who lived in his area. His name was Gary Leffew. Gary invited Richard to his professional bull-riding arena at his ranch. When Gary learnt that Richard had committed himself to a career as a bull rider, he agreed to help him. However, Gary told Richard that the first thing he would have to do is quit the amateur rodeo circuit. Gary said, "As long as you are hanging around amateurs, you will think like an amateur, and you will not improve your skills." That day Richard went from the top of the amateur bull riders to the bottom of the professionals.

After getting his professional cowboy association permit, Richard went back to Gary's rodeo arena, and he expected to get on some bulls. Much to Richard's surprise, Gary gave him a book when they met that day and sent him on his way. The book was *Psycho-Cybernetics* by Maxwell Maltz. Understandably for a cowboy, this was a major paradigm shift. All of the other seasoned bull riders had told Richard, "If you want to ride bulls, the secret is just getting on as many bulls as your body can withstand in terms of the pain." But they were not World Champion bull riders like his mentor was. So Richard took Gary's advice instead, and went home and read the book. When Richard finished, he went back to Gary, and couldn't believe what he did next, Gary gave Richard another book on thinking. A few more visits to Gary's ranch netted Richard more books. Richard said he read every one.

It is normal to think this is crazy, when all Richard wanted was to ride a bull. On one visit to Gary's, Richard finally mustered the courage to tell Gary he had read every book that he gave him, but now he wanted to get on some bulls. Gary explained to Richard, "Rich, before you ride bulls," and pointed to his head, "you've got to ride BULLS!" [meaning that the process of visualization had to come first, before action]. Now Richard understood that Gary was doing: preparing him mentally for riding bulls. "Okay," Richard told Gary, "so now that I've read all those books, I'm ready to get on a bull!" but he was wrong. The next step, Gary explained, was cassette tapes. Volumes of tapes!

When Gary finally said Richard was ready to get on a bull, it was a stationary barrel bull! There Richard learned how to visualize every bull movement and countermovement.

The next lesson Richard learned was about association. You cannot be the champion of the amateurs and be in their circles and expect to be professional. This is when Richard realised it was time to move from the amateur circuit and join the professional league, because professional champions think and act differently. "Who you hang around with," Gary explained, "can influence how you think." As Richard began travelling in the professional bull riders circuit, he said he learned that it was important to be with the riders who were winning. Richard recalled; "My mentor told me that if I couldn't find any winning bull riders to ride with, then I was to travel alone to protect my new winning mental attitude".

Richard went on to the world championship; though he did not win, he said he still did win a lot of rodeos, and he did make a lot of money riding in the professional bull-riding circuit. This cowboy eventually left the rodeo circuit and married a wonderful woman and they now own one of the largest employment agencies on the central coast of California. He said even now, he believes he is still thinking his way to the top. It is time to move from your current circles and locate a champions circuit to belong to.

Manage Your Relationships

Managing your relationships means you plan your relationships, you organize your relationships, control your relationships and lead your relationships. To plan your relationships means you are deliberate about who you associate with, you do not leave it to chance. Not everyone must be in your circle of relationships. This means you must have a general or rough criterion of who should be in your circle and the rest can be left to chance. You need a mastermind group or critical support group. People that help you with different aspects of life (Career, entertainment, relationship, financial management advice, investment, current affairs, fashion etc.).

To organize your relationship is to apportion roles for people you associate with and the lines they can cross or not cross. This should be done early enough in the relationship so that people do not cross lines. As relationships advance, expectations are formed based on previous interactions, which turn into social contracts and often become difficult to change without a conflict.

To control your relationships means you reflect and assess the relationship periodically to see if the relationship is serving the needed purpose or if it is toxic. Often you redirect relationships that are not serving your purpose to ensure that they work. In doing so, you also have to consider how you contributed to the situation and make the needed amends. It is said that when you find that you cannot change a situation, change yourself.

Shahida Arabi, bestselling author of *The Smart Girl's Guide to Self-Care* and many others has this advice: "When you notice someone does something toxic the first time, don't wait for the second time before you address it or cut them off. Many survivors are used to the 'wait and see' tactic which only leaves them vulnerable to a second attack. As your boundaries get stronger, the wait time gets shorter. You never have to justify your intuition."

To lead a relationship means you direct how the relationship should go, and this requires confidence in yourself. Relationships should be mutually beneficial. To lead your relationships means that you consciously direct how you want the relationship to go. You should not leave that to chance. You should take charge and direct which relationships should progress or be sustained, and those that you need to cut off, or those that you would like to slow down. You should decide whether or not a particular relationship is too toxic or not aligned to your personal values and principles. A young lady once shared with me that she had a friend she admired who was a little ahead in her career path. As the relationship gained grounds, the lady liked them to go out together over the weekends. One time, the lady called her while she was with me and she did not pick. I asked her to go ahead and take the call, but she said to me, I like and respect her so much, but she drinks alcohol too much and whenever we go out, she expects me to drink with her and if I don't, she makes it appear as though I am shy or not matured. But whenever I drink so much with her, I get headaches and feel sick. I asked, so why do you not insist on your way or will. I said to her what you friend is doing is leading the relationship because of the age difference but truth is you can also lead her. May be when you are bold and frank about why you do not like to take too much alcohol and the dangers associated with it, and you stand your grounds, she may follow your way. In that regards, you will be leading the relationship. She tried it and after some time, she called to thank me and said the lady now does not take alcohol at least in her presence.

When you leave your relationship to chance, it suggests lack of confidence in yourself due to the belief that the relationship is irreplaceable so others will direct the way the relationship should go for you, which can make you become a slave to that or in that relationship. Stephanie Perkins observes: "What we wait around a lifetime for with one person, we can find in a moment with someone else. Nothing is perfect. When you stop expecting people to be perfect, you can like them for who they are." But I add, it does not mean replace their life styles with yours.

Take charge of your relationships and manage them. Relationships come with communication and integrations which require time and sacrifices, but you do these thoughtfully, so your relationships do not become obstructive and detrimental to your purpose and meaning in life.

Understand your Environment and the Sources of Power

To navigate life's contours smoothly, you need to understand that you cannot do anything alone. From birth to death, we need people. People are the essence of your life and success. So how you manage people and the social capital you have is paramount to success. Every environment has its requirements, from legal, regulatory, technological and political requirements. Of all of these, the political requirement, which is the power that gets things done, is key to ascertain and understand. The political dynamics of an environment is not defined by those in political positions alone. In fact, there are some political figures who are pawns in the hands of master players. What is important is influence and aligning with those with influence is sheer wisdom for the smart. It is therefore important to know who the real players are. It could be a mistress, a security man or officer, a secretary, a personal assistant, a driver, a bodyguard a teacher, a friend, a parent or a colleague at work or school who have the influence over someone who can get things moving for you.

Even in conflict resolution, knowing someone with influence over the feuding party is helpful. Such people possess associate power or informational power or other sources of power which gives them influence. So political power and influence are not about position, they are about alignment. It is important that you form your own social capital around the sources of power. From positional power, to informational power, to associate power, to resource power or personal power. A woman I respect very highly once said, "to succeed, you've got to be a game player", but I say, you need to learn to play the game while keeping to your values and principles, and that requires flexibility with prudence. You must strike alliances that you can leverage. This means you find your way to associate with the movers and the shakers. Do not be timid, they are men and women like you, and blood flows through their veins just as butter melts in their mouths. Go to them. Tell them you want them to mentor you, or volunteer in an office you aspire to work in one day, join a network or club that have men and women of influence. These are a few strategies you could employ to have an effective social capital. Start to form your political and social network now.

CHAPTER 13

SPIRITUAL CAPITAL: LIFE BEYOND SELF AND A MEASURE OF YOUR ADVERSITY QUOTIENT

Success is falling nine times and getting up ten. Bon Jovi

WHAT IS SPIRITUALITY?

Many people confuse religion with spirituality, but the two are very different. Religion refers to a community or group that shares a specific set of organized beliefs and practices. Religion in my opinion is controlling belief in an object or superhuman that people worship and expect favour and protection from. In religion, people who share organized beliefs and practices often get together as a group to socialise, worship and exhort themselves. Religion can be regarded as a central and useful recourse for billions of people around the world. Author Jo Marchant, in his book *Cure,* reports that "there is evidence to suggest that being religious is good for health and that plenty of studies have linked a belief in God to favourable outcomes such as lower rates of heart disease, lower risk of high blood pressure, cancer as well as better outcomes in cases of HIV infections".[112] The focus of this chapter is however, on spirituality and not religion.

---

[112] Jo Marchant, 2017, Cure, A Journey into the science of mind over body, Retrieved June 21, 2021

Spirituality, on the other hand, is a personalised/individual practice that has to do with having a sense of ***purpose and peace***. Spirituality involves three things, which are an individual recognition and belief:

- that there is a course greater than oneself, something more to being human than sensory experience (like eating, sex, material possessions, feelings of looking good etc)
- that the greater whole of which we are part is controlled by something bigger than man.
- that peace will always prevail no matter the challenges (faith)

Your spirituality therefore means that you recognise that your life has significance that goes beyond your routine everyday experiences that feed your biological and sensory needs, which often drive selfishness, aggression and competition. Secondly, it also means that you understand that your life is a significant part of a purposeful existence in our universe.[113] Spirituality therefore starts with understanding your significance and purpose in life, a piece in the puzzle, without you, the puzzle cannot be complete. Locating your own place in the puzzle may help other pieces to fit or find their own places. Aside from thinking about yourself and your significance, spirituality is how you think about others and the connection between your life and that of others. Thirdly, being spiritual means, you have a belief or faith that no matter what the challenges of life may be, you will always find peace in the end, which helps you stay calm in challenging times. The two key indicators of spirituality are therefore ***purpose and peace.***

Since spirituality has to do with your purpose and significance, it should be the main measure of your success in life. This is because when all is done, your spirituality should be a measure of whether your mission in life has been accomplished or not. Success can therefore be considered both the intended and unintended consequence of your spirituality, which is your impact in life due to your response to your bigger calling to a purposeful life in pursuit of personal and common good.

---

[113] Maya Spencer, 2012, What is Spirituality? A Personal Exploration, https://www.rcpsych.ac.uk/docs/default-source/members/sigs/spirituality-spsig/what-is-spirituality-maya-spencer-x.pdf?sfvrsn=f28df052_2

WHAT IS SPIRITUAL CAPITAL?

Spiritual capital is the extra-personal *wealth of an individual.* It is the ability to be purposeful and persevere for results through the exercise of faith. It is a measure of our purpose and faith in action. It is that characteristic that helps us to see and think beyond ourselves in a purpose driven life and to keep persevering in the face of adversity. Our spiritual capital is a measure of our connectedness to the world and our belief system that helps us to hold faith in the face of difficulties. Faith, according to the Apostle Paul in the Bible, is our belief to see the evidence of the things we hope for and to hold the substance of the things not yet seen, as if they were real in our minds. The practice of using our minds to control and call things there that do not yet exist into being for our benefit and the benefit of others is our spiritual capital. It keeps us going in the face of obstacles.

Spiritual Capital therefore relates to our deep feelings about our purpose and confidence in that purpose. It relates to our ability to fulfil our contribution to society, our connectedness with others, and the feeling of assurance or confidence that positive things will come our way no matter the challenges. It is the hope that allows us to turn obstacles into opportunities for the benefit of self and others.

Developing Our Spiritual Capital

Developing our spiritual capital involves:

- Purpose Thinking
- Systems Thinking
- Positive Thinking

PURPOSE THINKING

Purpose thinking refers to our concern and commitment to a mission in life. Knowing and being deliberate about what we believe we exist to do, how we identify what we exist to do, and what actually makes us unique and fulfilled in life. Sometimes, our focus is very different from our actual purpose in life. When that happens, we miss what we are called to do by life and causes us to struggle a lot in our pursuit or career. Often what we are called to do comes to us with ease and joy because we have the talents and passion for them. To know whether we are doing what we are called to do by life, we need to answer the following questions:

1. What is your purpose in life? Have you located it, and if so, what do you exist to do and who do you exist to serve?
2. What talents do I have, and what do people praise me for?
3. What am I good at, or what are my strengths and weaknesses?
4. What are my opportunities to use my strengths or talents, and what challenges may I face using those talents?
5. What Skills do I need to develop to make my talents blossom?
6. What makes you unique in fulfilling your purpose and passion in life?
7. What do you want to be remembered for and what will you actually be remembered for if you look at your life today?
8. What legacies and memories will be associated with your name or presence?

The answers to these questions will help you identify your mission or purpose in life. You could also identify your purpose by the things people tell you that you are good at, or things you do with ease. To locate your purpose, you need to understand your personality. If you have not yet taken a personality test, please do. There are several personality tests that can help you understand your personality. I find Myers Briggs type indicator quite useful. Visit https://www.16personalities.com/free-personality-test or search the web for other personality tests. Many are free.

Understanding your personality and your purpose is the root of all your endeavours in life. When you think about your purpose, do not look at it only from a short-term perspective, but from a long-term or strategic and generational point. Being purposeful means that we are mindful about the fact that our choices, actions and inactions affect others and can affect generations unborn. For example, Alfred Nobel instituted the Nobel Prizes for the greatest benefits to humankind. Some people create value and wealth for generations to come, while others think only about what is in it for them now, tomorrow can take care of itself. Such selfish thoughts are not purpose thinking. When you do things that will inure to the benefit of others and the universe at large, we are actually living our purpose.

Alfred Nobel may have made some mistakes in life, but he did not dwell on his mistakes. Rather, purpose thinking made him think through his purpose and what he would be remembered for, thus he created the Nobel Prize, which has promoted peace and supported human wellbeing for over a century.[114]

On the 27th of November 1895, Alfred Nobel, a Swedish chemist, engineer, industrialist and inventor of dynamite, left $9 million in his will to establish the Nobel Prizes after having been condemned for profiting from the sales of arms. He stipulated that the awards be given annually, disregarding the nationality of possible recipients. He also specified six areas to be covered by the rewards; namely Peace, Literature, Physics, Chemistry and Physiology or Medicine. In 1968, the Bank of Sweden added the award for economic science in memory of Nobel.[115] Nobel's family were surprised and upset that he had not left all of his fortune to them, but rather to establish the prizes. Although they contested the will, his last wishes were respected and the first Nobel Prizes were awarded in 1901, on the 5-year anniversary of his death.[116] Many great persons who impacted the world with what they shared have since received these prizes.

Wangarĩ Muta Maathai was a Kenyan social, environmental, and political activist (1st April 1940 – 25th September 2011) and the first African woman to win the Nobel Peace Prize. In 1977, Maathai founded the Green Belt Movement, a non-governmental, environmental organization focused on the planting of trees, environmental conservation, and women's rights. In 1984, she was awarded the Right Livelihood Award for "converting the Kenyan ecological debate into mass action for reforestation".

Rev. Martin Luther King Jr. became the youngest person to receive the Nobel Peace Prize at 35 years old when his work to end racial discrimination in the United States through non-violent means was recognized in 1964.

---

[114] https://www.nobelprize.org/education-network-nobel-prize-teacher-summit/ retrieved 18th August, 2021

[115] *"Alfred Nobel's Fortune"*. The Norwegian Nobel Committee. Archived from *the original* on 6 January 2017. *Retrieved 22 May, 2021.*

[116] Alfred Nobel's Will". The Norwegian Nobel Committee. Retrieved 29 March 2021

Mother Teresa blessed the world with her love from 1910 to 1997. She was, a Roman Catholic nun of Albanian ethnicity and Indian citizenship who founded the Missionaries of Charity in Calcutta, India, in 1950. She spent the next 45 years ministering to the poor, sick, orphaned and dying, while overseeing the Missionaries of Charity's gradual expansion throughout and beyond India. At the time of her death in 1997, there were 610 missions in 123 countries, including hospices and homes for people with HIV, leprosy and tuberculosis; soup kitchens; children's and family counselling programmes; orphanages and schools. Mother Teresa won the Nobel Peace Prize in 1979. Following her death, she was beatified by Pope John Paul II, made a saint and given the title Blessed Teresa of Calcutta. Mother Teresa observed: "Let us not be satisfied with just giving money. Money is not enough, money can be got, but they need your hearts to love them. So, spread your love everywhere you go."

Desmond Tutu is another Nobel Peace Prize winner, in 1984 the well-known campaigner against apartheid also tried to tackle issues such as AIDS in Africa and received a Nobel Prize. Florence Nightingale (1820 – 1910) was a nurse who helped to standardize and improve the quality of nursing in Nineteenth Century Britain. She came to be known as the mother of modern nursing.

Sir Alexander Fleming and his team of scientists (Ernest Chain and Sir Howard Florey) won the 1945 Nobel Prize in Physiology or Medicine for their discovery of penicillin, a fungus, that is used as an antibiotic. Fleming discovered the antibiotic effect of the fungus by chance on his return from holiday in August 1928 when he discovered that a fungus had developed in a stack of Petri dishes containing bacteria he had left in the laboratory. He observed that the bacteria in the dishes immediately surrounding the fungus had died, while bacteria in the dishes farther away were unaffected, so he followed his curiosity to find out whether the fungus killed the bacteria. Fleming focused on investigating this observation for decades, and eventually, together with his team, isolated "penicillin", an antibiotic named after the fungus' genus (Penicillium). Penicillin as we know it cures infections, scarlet fever, gonorrhoea, pneumonia, meningitis, diphtheria, syphilis and other serious infectious diseases, and has helped many people. Fleming did not only think about himself in his decades of pursuit to make penicillin available to the world. Fleming shared his knowledge with the world.

Albert Einstein, considered by many as the most famous scientist in the history of the world, also won the Nobel Prize in Physics in 1921 for discovering the cause of the "photoelectric effect." This phenomenon revealed that when atoms are bombarded with light, they emit electrons. In 1905, Einstein argued that light was divided into discrete packets (which we now call photons). Einstein's painstaking research ended in his legacies and the recognition of his contribution. Today, it is clear that Einstein, Fleming, and the others did not live for themselves alone but dedicated their time to contribute to the welfare of humanity and generations. These Nobel Prize winners, like many others, understood their purpose in life through the responsibility they bore towards other people who knowingly or unknowingly waited for their services and contributions. Such are the examples of people who cared and shared their lives and heart, so others will have a better life. This is why their memories are honoured for their contributions.

What are you living for, and for whom? What are you sharing with the world, your country and community? Often what we share with the world makes a life that goes beyond us and not just a living for us.

SYSTEMS THINKING

Systems thinking refers to how we think our purpose and survival depends on others and how others also depend on us for survival. It is about interdependency. A system is a set of interrelated components that work together in a particular environment to perform whatever functions are needed to achieve the objectives of that environment.[117]

Systems thinking, in my opinion, is a holistic approach to thinking about the interconnectedness of components in the environment (people, processes and things etc) and how to make those components work together over time and within the larger context to create new value that can benefit that whole environment. This means whatever actions you take or actions

---

[117] Loyla Acaroglu, 2017, Tools for Systems Thinkers: The 6 Fundamental Concepts of Systems Thinking, a quote from Danella Meadows, https://medium.com/disruptive-design/tools-for-systems-thinkers-the-6-fundamental-concepts-of-systems-thinking-379cdac3dc6a, retrieved 15th April, 2021

you refuse to take, you have to think about the consequences that decision will have on you, other people, and things in the environment. Here you should consider what positive things can emerge and what negative things can emerge. Seeking feedback and assessing our actions from time to time is a good way in systems thinking to know how your actions and inactions are affecting people and things in the environment.

Systems thinking involves a belief and attitude that personal success comes from service to others and the universe. Systems thinking will ask, how will this affect others? Will this help someone or put a smile on somebody's face today? It is often said that sharing is caring, and caring is divine. Caring for others is like planting seeds which you harvest later in many forms. Caring about others helps us to think ethically about our choices and actions, particularly the consequences of our actions on other people or things in the systems, whether legal or illegal. Theodore Roosevelt once said "Nobody cares how much you know until they know how much you care. Sarah Williams, author of the article *Sharing is Caring: 6 Scientifically Proven Ways Helping Others Can Improve Your Life* notes:

"I've come to believe that the simple formula for happiness and success in life lies in caring about others, helping them in any way we can, and sharing what we have. I learned this the hard way. In the beginning, when I was striving for career success, better relationships, improved overall health and mental well-being, I thought others had nothing to do with it, that it's a battle I had to win on my own. With this mindset, though, I made my life more complicated and didn't improve personally, spiritually, or professionally any time soon. Then, I decided to give another approach a try. To make others part of my journey in small ways but do it every day. I began talking to both strangers and people in my surroundings more, opening up, receiving feedback, sharing my goals and giving others advice, or simply listening to their problems and showing compassion. I stopped investing my time only in 'me' activities and began doing 'we' activities. That could be seeing someone in need and spending time with them even if I didn't feel like it (not within my productive routine), becoming more active in the local community, volunteering even. All that paid off tenfold because I received so much in return that my career, happiness level, relationships and peace of mind were all improving. After experiencing the wonderful benefits of helping others, Sarah also learnt that science backs some of the benefits she had experienced." [118]

In business, it is the idea of substituting the common bottom line "Profits" with enlightened shareholder value, where we think of the interconnectedness of our actions to all stakeholders, including the environment, reflects systems thinking. One reason for the spiritual growth we experience as a result of giving more and thinking of the consequences of our actions on others is that as we give, we find meaning and fulfilment that helps to fill the void inside us, making us more confident, and boosting our self-esteem.[119]

However, it is important to recognize that while thinking of our connectedness in the universe and helping others, we do not do it to the detriment of what we stand for (our purpose and values) or what we are working very hard to build. It is important to recognise causes of actions on behalf of others that can affect our mission or purpose. The story of the Light Housekeeper and the Krupp Story mentioned in this book, are typical examples. Systems thinking also means we are investing time, energy and resources in things that can transcend us and live beyond us. It also means thinking of the consequences of our actions on other people including generations unborn and the environment.

Positive Thinking

If you do not have faith in yourself and faith in something bigger than you, it is difficult to ascend the climb and achieve your goals, aspirations and plans. In climbing the ladder of life, we often get confronted with frustrations, we fail, we fall and get bruised. We experience resistance to our values of integrity, honesty, transparency and citizenship behaviours. We often get to the cross-roads, where we get confronted with the dilemmas of life. It is during such difficult times in our lives that our spiritual capital is

---

[118] WebMD, 2005, What is Cortisol? https://www.webmd.com/a-to-z-guides/what-is-cortisol2005, retrieved 31st March, 2021

[119] Sarah Williams, December 2019, Sharing is Caring: 6 Scientifically Proven Ways Helping Others Can Improve Your Life, https://addicted2success.com/life/sharing-is-caring-6-scientifically-proven-ways-helping-others-can-improve-your-life/, retrieved 31st March, 2021

called to work. Leadership and the climb are not for the faint-hearted and yet not for the foolhardy. It is for the prudent. The climb is for they who muster the skills of *courage, patience, understanding and resilience.*

It gets to a point where your personal, human, and social capital fail you because men cannot help you, and you cannot help yourself, because your *know-what, know-how* and *who* you know cannot help you. When your three capitals fail, it is then that you call in the master capital, your spiritual capital. It is at this point in your life's journey, along the climb, that your spiritual capital is brought to the task. When things do not seem to be working as expected, when the political and regulatory mechanisms get in your way to undermine your purpose or investments, or your business, when a pandemic forces your course of action to change, or compels you to change your goals among other challenges, when crisis hits us so hard and we look for something to hold on to or to lean on, then we shout out to our spiritual capital to come in and save us. Then our faith comes in to give us hope to carry on. It is in such challenging times that we begin to see reason why Voltaire said, "If God did not exist, it would be necessary to invent him". [120] As humans, we cannot predict the future with accuracy, so we need something bigger than us to put our trust in. Some call the bigger thing we can trust in the transcendent or God, and I call it God. *We need faith to hold onto hope which comforts us and tells us not to worry and assures us that the crisis will soon be over and better things will come our way, no matter how tough or gloomy the situation may be.* Spiritual capital in this respect relates to your deep feelings of intuition, beliefs and faith in something bigger than yourself that helps you in times of challenge, obstacles, frustrations, adversity or crisis to keep going.

Our spiritual capital is therefore expressed in our response (not reactions) to situations that appear frustrating. It is what keeps us calm in crisis-like situations, because we have a backbone and an unseen pillar within us to lean on. This can be an inner fortitude, expressed in our resilience to situations. I noted with surprise that many top businessmen

---

[120] Voltaire [1768], Epître à l'auteur du livre des Trois imposteurs (OEuvres complètes de Voltaire, ed. Louis Moland [Paris: Garnier, 1877-1885], tome 10, pp. 402-405)
https://www.whitman.edu/VSA/trois.imposteurs.html, retrieved 31st March, 2021

and politicians who may appear to be atheists have belief systems, spiritual fathers and spiritual masters who they consult before major actions or decisions. I consult Jehovah, the unseen God, in him, my personal faith and resilience is built, through my master Jesus and his word as contained in the Bible. What about you? What gives you strength to fight battles that tend to overwhelm you.

It is indeed when the going gets tough, when we are at our wits end, when we get to the crossroads and have no one to turn to, that we know that if there were no God, it might well be necessary for man to invent one, that prayer and faith shines some light on our path. Prayer or faith (or both) work to spread tranquillity and psychological comfort in the soul in times of difficulty that you cannot find in any other act. It is through our spiritual capital that our passion and determination is sharpened to help us to move on.[121]

Faith reassures us that it is not as bad as you sometimes think it is. It is during the dark times of life that you need to whisper to yourself, "Don't worry, it shall be well", that your faith is deployed. Once your faith gets to work, you soon realise all works out well in the end because faith comes in to fill the void and gets you to move on with confidence into the future, often without realising how it happened. That is your spiritual capital, a measure of your adversity quotient. When you make declarations and things work for you, it is your spiritual capital at work. The more of it you have, the better your "Execution Capital" and ability to use your human capital and social capital to work for you.[47] Below are some steps to practice your spiritual capital:

- Get your purpose and mission in life defined.
- Develop a vision
- Develop Faith. Faith begins and works through visualization of a desired state, so you have to first visualize the desired state (vision)
- Articulate the desired state or vision and goals and make spoken declarations. Write the vision down and speak it out to yourself. Be mindful who you share spiritual things with because spirituality is an individual engagement and not everyone should hear of

---

[121] The School of Life, https://www.theschooloflife.com/thebookoflife/voltaire/ Retrieved 2Oth March, 2021

your plans or vision, evil imaginations can ambush your dreams, though they may not be able to kill them.

- Develop a plan with the goals for your vision
- Take actions directed towards the vision with purpose and confidence
- Know when to negotiate, when to collaborate, when to accommodate, when to compromise, when to compete, and when to fight for your vision and goals. Always keep in mind, it is better to have something than nothing at all, provided that something does not end up being counter-productive when striving to achieve your purpose.
- When obstacles, challenges or crises emerge, do not fizzle out, turn your faith on and show your adversity quotient by remaining resilient. It is, however, important to know when and how to quit, so you can redirect yourself towards the purpose.

Finishing the Goal is Hard, Giving up is Easy so You need an Anchor

The biggest regret in life is not doing what you were called to do on earth, or not doing it to the best of your abilities. The regret of not knowing what you could have accomplished because you were too scared or didn't work hard enough, or gave up when it got tough, can be painful. Whatever the goal, whether a professional goal or a business goal, or fitness goal, or sports goal, try to push it through. It is, however, important to know when to change a course of action, while staying to the purpose.

As motivational speaker Ross Perot said, "Most people give up just when they're about to achieve success. They give up at the last minute of the game, one foot from a winning touchdown." To succeed and climb up, you need that insatiable desire for fulfilment, then success and growth will follow the pursuit. But the climb is not without its trials. Several perils accompany the quest for the prize. In other words, there are several dangers associated with attaining something of value, and a price must be paid for the prize. Often the bigger the prize, the more the perils and the higher the price to pay. So, the bigger the prize, the higher the sacrifice. That is why you need purpose, focus, toughness and agility to succeed. In some instances, you need some roughness to sail through. PERSEVERANCE is the key quality of climbers and success. Several factors (interests of the powers that be, regulatory manipulations, natural crisis, financial crisis, family issues, ill health, disengagement of helpers or investors, changes in business environment, competitor manoeuvres among other) could hinder your pursuit. Yet you need the psychological toughness and preparedness to move forward. The world abounds with success stories of faith, perseverance and success my own to start with.

SAY TO YOURSELF, YES, I CAN: BUT IT TAKES CRAZY FAITH

Becoming a University Professor

As I already mentioned in an earlier chapter, I was born in Accra and grew up in Nungua, in the Greater Accra Region of Ghana. My father was a middle class civil engineer and a university graduate, and my mother a beautician. My father made me understand that a university degree was my gateway to success in life. My goal was to get a university degree for whatever purpose. After my Common Entrance examination, I was rejected by all of my three choices of secondary schools, so I ended up in a rural secondary school. Later on, I moved on to Nungua Secondary School, where I studied for my GCE Ordinary Level (O'Level) certificate. Again, my choice of school for my Advance Level Certificate (A 'Level) refused my admission initially, but I persisted, and I got into that choice school, which was St. Mary's Secondary School in Accra. Even though the odds were very much against my admission, my faith assured me that I would get into St. Mary's, irrespective of the fact all hopes seemed to have been lost on that.

When we first went to follow up on my A-level admissions, the then headmistress did not even offer us a chair. While standing, behind the door in her little squeezed office, she said to me and my mum, people with your kind of grades are not accepted into this school and immediately rang the bell for the secretary. Leaving her office was a task. Feeling so disappointed, I decide to go myself to see the then Regional Director for Education (Mrs. Margaret Quist of blessed Memory) to tell her about my plight and dream to enter an all-girls school, in this case St. Mary's

Secondary School at the age of 17. Mrs. Quist gave me her assurances, and happily and confidently gave me a note to the headmistress of St. Mary's Secondary School, who also happened to be her neighbour. This offered me a second opportunity to meet with the headmistress of St. Mary's School for my admission. This time, filled with confidence, we took the note to the headmistress. With so much disregard, she said to us at the reception, I told you young lady, people with your kind of grades are not accepted here. Go look for your placement from the government. Students like you who get rejected by your choice schools are accepted by other schools during selection. Certainly, do not come back here, because we have no place for you. I followed, her advice and went to the selection centre and discovered that I had been accepted by Ofori Panyin Secondary School in the Eastern Region of Ghana. My father took me to Ofori to get my prospectus and to get ready for school. At this point, school had already been reopened two weeks earlier. We were well received by the Headmaster of Ofori Panyin Secondary. Ofori Panyin was a mixed School with a very beautiful campus, much nicer than St. Mary's at the time, but I still wanted to attend St. Mary's.

At this point though, I had received the prospectus for Ofori Panyin Secondary and I was preparing to go there, I was still dreaming, about St. Mary's. I saw myself twice in my dreams wearing the St. Mary's Secondary School uniform and interacting with fellow students in that school. Now my trunk and chop-boxes were packed for Ofori Pinyin Secondary, but I still believed that my boxes were packed for St. Mary's. The eve before I was to leave for Ofori Panyin, I was preparing my black pepper sauce, which was to be the last to go into my chopbox. Black pepper sauce (Shito) is a traditional delicacy that almost all students take to the boarding school in Ghana. The pepper sauce was still simmering on the stove and was almost done, it was around 5.30 pm, and my mother jokingly said, "oh Ofori Panyin here we come". Then I retorted frantically, Mummy, mummy please this pepper is not going to Ofori Panyin it is going to St. Mary's. My mummy, shocked by what she had just heard, shook her head slowly and told me I must be crazy. "You must be hallucinating, better get used to the idea that you are going to Ofori Panyin." About 20 minutes later, the phone rang, it was the Headmistress of St. Mary's, Secondary School, she said, "Can I speak to Ms. Goski Nee-whang please?

I said speaking mum. She said "you are expected to report at St. Mary's Secondary School tomorrow by 7.30am. I left the phone handle hanging and started screaming, mummy, mummy, I made it. Yes, I, made it to St. Mary's. You can imagine my joy of achieving what I dreamt about. My crazy faith got me to St. Mary's. I was SUCCESSFUL in getting to St. Mary's Secondary School.

But, history will repeat itself. Again, after my GCE Advanced Level (A'Levels) examination, my results would not allow me entry into the university to do the programme of my choice because of one bad grade, but I did not give up. I was so disappointed in myself at my grades that I felt sick, I lost my balance and could not walk or sit. I was hospitalized for three months. One of my friends who visited me while in hospital later told me, "oh Goski, I thought you would not make it." What kept me going was my faith. I had learnt already that faith makes a way, where there is no way. I was poised to enter the university, no matter the impediment. I stayed home for a year after my A-level National Service. During this period, I pressed hard to gain admissions to the Kwame Nkrumah University for Science and Technology, but was not successful for the course I wanted. I was still positive that I would go to the university, no matter what it took. One day, I saw an advert in the Daily Graphic Newspaper that the University of Cape-Coast was accepting people with my kind of grades for a six-week bridging course, after which they would take examinations for selection. I said Bingo. This is my chance. I hurriedly got myself ready and the very next day I was on my way to Cape-Coast. I successfully went through the process, and that is how I got admitted to the University of Cape Coast to do a Bachelor of Science degree in Chemistry and a Diploma in Education concurrently.

I finished my entire undergraduate programme without having to trail a course. I followed up immediately to obtain a Master's of Philosophy in Food Science at the University of Ghana, a Doctorate of Business Administration from the Swiss Management Centre, and a Doctorate of Philosophy (Ph.D.) in Business Administration from the Central University of Nicaragua. Now, I am a full professor and one of Africa's leading experts in Quality Management with a focus on leadership of international repute. In June 2019, I was "the keynote speaker who delivered the prestigious Oxford University's Sir David Watson Memorial Lecture at the Human

Welfare Conference. (https://www.gtc.ox.ac.uk/news-and-events/events-series/human-welfare-conference/human-welfare-conference-2019/2019-david-watson-memorial-lecturer-professor-mrs-goski-alabi/).

I am currently, the President of the African Council for Distance Education (ACDE), and Chair of the African Network for Internationalisation of Education (ANIE). I was also founding Dean of the School of Research and Graduate Studies of the University of Professional Studies in Ghana, and founder and president of Laweh University College, the first accredited Open university in Ghana, and second in West Africa. I am also author of the seminal book *Managing for Excellence in the 21ˢᵗ Century, the Total Quality Approach,* which appeared in the New York Times in August 2017. https://www.amazon.com/Managing-Excellence-Twenty-First-Century-Approach/dp/1524643246.

I have spoken at many international conference and fora, including four times national delegate to the World Health Assembly, served on ISO and Codex Committees, the Women's Economic Forum, consulted for many organizations including the European Union as a Framework Consultant for the Pesticides initiative Programme, served as lead in a number of national and international projects including the World Bank, DFID, DAAD among many others. I have served on a number of international and National Boards and Committees, including chairperson of the interim Council of the Accra College of Education, the oldest Government Post-Secondary Institution in Ghana and I am now an acclaimed academic and entrepreneur, receiving Africa's Most Respected CEO Award in Dubai by the Business Executive Magazine among many others. All of these would not have been possible without crazy faith, a measure of my spiritual capital. Like Einstein, I had to prove to myself that yes, I, can. If you believe in yourself, and say to yourself yes you can, you will make it, no matter the obstacles.

The Little Story of Faith Also Worked For My Niece

About 20 years after that positive experience of faith getting into St. Mary's Secondary School, I told the story to my niece, who wanted to go to Aburi Girls Secondary, but landed at Akosombo Secondary, an equally good school. After completing a year out of her 3 years in Akosombo Senior

High School, she thought it was impossible to switch school without losing a year. I told her about my experience with practising positive thinking, and that if she would believe and exercise crazy faith like I did, she too can get into her dream school. She responded, while sobbing, and said "but Auntie, my situation is different." I then responded, "yes, but it does not matter, if only you can believe, and imagine yourself in Aburi Girls High School, and declare that I will be in Aburi Girls, it does not matter what it takes, you will find yourself there without losing a year."

Coincidentally, my husband had a meeting with the headmistress that had nothing to do with my niece's admission. My husband called to tell me, and I pleaded that he seizes the opportunity to discuss our niece's admission, and before we knew it, my niece was accepted to Aburi Girls Secondary School, without losing a year. Before leaving for Aburi Girls, I asked her, 'do you remember our discussion about exercising crazy faith?" We both laughed and gave a hi-five to that. Your passion and crazy faith will make a way for you when there seem to be no way. Passion and faith can help you turn your obstacles into opportunities. I do not know how, but it works. Indeed, faith moves mountains, and with purpose and passion, sets you up for success.

MALALA: A CLASSICAL EXAMPLE OF DUAL PERSPECTIVE OF SPIRITUALITY AND SUCCESS

In an interview, Malala said "I think death did not want to kill me, and God was with me, and the people prayed."

Malala was sixteen when she was nominated for the Nobel Peace Prize for her advocacy for equal opportunities for girl education in Pakistan, which made her a target for assassination. In an interview, she describes the reason she survived the Bullet and made the statement above. Here is the story.

Two men approached a Pakistani school bus. One of them climbed onto the bus and asked, "who is Malala?" Malala did not remember what happened next, but her friend describes the moment when they shot her at very close range. Scientists are unable to explain how one could survive such an attack. She bled profusely and was in critical condition, but two hours later, a helicopter took her from the local hospital to a Military Surgeon. The surgeon spent five hours trying to remove the swelling from her brain and remove tiny clots. The strange coincidence was that, this was someone in Pakistan for the first time, a top specialist in paediatric trauma surgeon from England, Dr. Phiona Reynolds, and her colleague Dr. Yanin Kiani, who were in governmental meetings discussing global medical programmes, when suddenly, Dr. Reynolds was told she was urgently needed to save the life a dying heroine.

The tubes had given Malala an infection, her blood was not clotting, her lungs and kidneys were beginning to fail. She had become septic. It was obvious she had a life-threatening infection, Doctor Reynolds observed. Weighing the odds, Dr, Reynolds made a risky recommendation to take the seriously ill Malala on an eight-hour trip to a high-tech hospital in England. Can Malala survive? Something more powerful than anyone could explain was working for Malala and the world prayed for her survival. The Emir of the United Arab Emirates made an astonishing offer, one of his royal planes with a state-of-the-art medical facility for the entire eight-hour trip. Dr. Reynolds and her colleague kept Malala alive breath by breath, organ by organ. They also noted something that defied possibility, the bullet took a path that simply could not be believed". In Dr. Reynolds' own words, "The chances of being shot at point-blank range and that happened I don't know, but it is amazing, truly amazing, I do not know why she survived." A bullet travelling 1000 feet per second hit Malala, slipped under Malala's skin, and hit the skull, but as it headed towards the brain, that bone was so hard and curved that it forced the bullet to deviate from its course and smash her ear drum, sever a nerve in her face, and hit her shoulder. The two Medical Doctors considered the fact that she did not die on the spot or shortly after a miracle. Malala believed God saved her. The Doctors were still not sure whether she would be able to see, or walk, or speak again. However, to everyone's surprise, moments after her eyes opened, she could use a letter board to spell out the words 'country' and 'father'. For three more months, Malala received treatment and surgery to reconnect the nerve in her face. Malala said, "I think Death did not want to kill me, and God was with me, and people prayed for me. I woke up 10 days later in a hospital in Birmingham, England. The doctors and nurses told me about the attack — and that people around the world were praying for my recovery."

HOPE RESTS IN YOU AND IN SOMETHING BEYOND YOU

Believe in Yourself, Believe in God

Nigerian musician Burna Boy grabbed the Best Global Music Album at the 63rd Grammy Award in the month of March 2021 for his 'Twice As Tall' single, which was released in 2020. His singles had been nominated twice for the Grammy in 2020 and 2021 but won in 2021. Speaking of his award, he said "This is a big win to my generation of Africans all over the world, and a lesson to every African out there, no matter where you are, no matter what you plan to do you can achieve it, no matter where you are from because you are a king, just believe in yourself."[122] However, taking to twitter he said "God is definitely not a man, I will never forget how many of you prayed that I don't win, too dumb to understand that you also win when I win, No worry, this is just the beginning. God is Great."[123] Burna Boy's response to his win clearly shows how far he has come and the fact that to succeed we need to believe in ourselves in whatever pursuit we undertake, but also believe in God to put the Nay-Sayers to shame. The fact that Burna Boy had to drop out of university, did not mean he could not shine in another field. He only had to locate his passion and purpose and stay focused on that, while believing in himself and God.

REJECTION MAY BE YOUR ROAD TO LOCATING VOCATION

Good luck they say counts towards the road to success but not without the bad. Jack Ma is the richest man in Asia (worth about $39 Billion) and runs one of the largest companies in China, Alibaba.[124] However, Jack Ma did not start as a genius. Alibaba was a result of his pursuit to do something meaningful in his life. He faced rejection much of his work life before he

---

[122] SABC News Nigeria's Burna Boy says Grammy win marks 'big moment' for African music, 22 March 2021
https://www.sabcnews.com/sabcnews/nigerias-burna-boy-says-grammy-win-marks-big-moment-for-african-music/ Reuters, retrieved 22nd March 2021

[123] BBC 21st Mach, 2021Burna Boy: I deserve to win the Gammy< https://www.bbc.com/pidgin/media-56473931, retrieved 22 March, 2021

[124]

created Alibaba. He applied for 30 different jobs including the police and KFC and was rejected. In addition, he applied and got denied 10 different times from Harvard. But, after discovering his purpose in internet business in the mid 90's, he understood the possibilities that existed. He went on to create several companies despite all the rejection he had previously faced.

If Jack had listened to others and let their rejections influence him, he would have accepted all the rejection and lived a life of mediocrity, self-pity and regret. Rather than feel dejected about his rejections and failure, he kept exploring new opportunities until he found a place in the internet business which has impacted millions of lives around the globe and still does. Ironically, Jack Ma had to do a commencement speech at Harvard, from where he was rejected 10 times. My lesson from Ma is to look for opportunities connected to our interest and not to give up until you get fulfilment. Alibaba turned his test into a testimony as Dinah Hamilton the Ghanaian Gospel singer puts it. Faith indeed, makes Perseverance rewarding.

Success has Seasons but no Timelines: Exercise Patience while Remaining Focused and Disciplined

I have selected four examples of people whose success stories demonstrate that Success has its own seasons, but no timelines. We could achieve it in the time we have planned but, success does not always follow our plans.

- ### *McDonald's – Ray Croc*

McDonald's would not have been a global chain if it were not for the perseverance of Ray Croc.

Ray was over 50 and a struggling milkshake machine salesman who lived a comfortable life but craved more. He met the brothers behind McDonald's and eventually convinced them of a franchise model to grow the brand. This led him to massive expansion, which grew into the McDonald's we know today. McDonald's $27 billion in revenue makes it the 90th-largest economy in the world.

- ### *Thomas Edison*

Thomas Edison is the definition of perseverance. Considered unteachable at a young age, the inventor went on to eventually create the electric light bulb. While most thought he "failed" he simply said he found over 1,000 ways not to build a light bulb. He did get it finally, demonstrating that there was no timer on success.

- ### *Colonel Sanders*

Colonel Sanders founded KFC when he was about 60 years old after receiving his first social security check. Yet, it was the beginning of another global success story, of a man in pursuit of rendering service, irrespective of age. I am not sure Colonel Sanders anticipated or even aimed for a global scale success like the KFC we know today, yet his actions and persistence allowed success to ensue. Working from 60 to 73 years old, Sanders honed his technique and grew his business. With hard work and passion for serving, he made it. At the time of giving up the business, he sold the company for $2 million and lived out the rest of his life in comfort, not needing to depend on his social security check. He knew when to stop. Sometimes knowing when to move on and when to stop brings success because success has seasons but no timelines.

- ### *WhatsApp – Jan Koum*

Jan Koum is the founder of WhatsApp which sold to Facebook for 19 billion dollars. He grew up very poor in Ukraine and didn't even have running water. After working for Yahoo until 2007, he applied to Facebook, but could not make it at the last stage of interview. He was part of the "Facebook reject club," as Forbes described it. Instead of brooding over his rejection, Jan went on to establish WhatsApp in February 2009. Before WhatsApp, Jan lost a couple of jobs, but was focused. He stumbled upon the idea of WhatsApp and went all out. That was his season and his time. It did not matter what he went through. The important point is that he is now a billionaire, and his WhatsApp is connecting people around the world. Jan's is a case of hard work, patience and perseverance. To achieve success in life, do not dwell on your past, rather focus on the now and the future. Do not let your past define you, focus on your future. Never give up.

Lessons from the Stories Shared So Far

The stories shared so far teach us about handling rejection, uncertainty, challenges and crises as key aspects of the road to success. Those who often emerge successful are those who are able to manage challenges successfully. This requires a high level of spiritual capital. Sometimes we doubt ourselves, other times, people doubt us and there are many nay-sayers around who may discourage you when they hear of your aspirations and plans. Often, people do not see what you see because it is your vision not theirs, their position and comments should only help you refine your ideas, not kill your vision.

So, you need to find any means possible to make things happen, not because you want to prove anyone wrong, but because you believe in your vision and your goals. For this reason, you need to exercise faith, which requires a very positive mind and a positive attitude. Many call it ***positive thinking***. It is the ability to see hope when many others see obstacles or impossibilities. The ability to have a problem-solving mindset and attitude goes a long way to make us successful in our pursuit for fulfilment. The ability to hold on to the vision and goals without giving up but changing the approach (strategy) where needed is a measure of your spiritual capital. Though exercising hope can cause some pain and emotional stress because it requires patience, once you accomplish the goals and you are successful, you will have the satisfaction of fulfilment, irrespective of where you started from. The Outcome of genuine achievement will be the happiness you so well deserve. This is why success should not be the pursuit, but rather fulfilment.

Just like Positive Thinking, ***Perseverance in the Face of Adversity*** is another principle for success. Success is not designed to be easy, otherwise all men would be successful. Don't quit when obstacles arise. Press on but know when to change your strategy and have faith in yourself and your vision until it's accomplished. Like Frankl said, "that which must give light, must endure burning". The higher the prize, the bigger the price, perils and sacrifices.

The stories of perseverance shared in this book show that human beings are capable of anything with hard work, discipline, faith and belief in themselves.

Never give up on your plans, keep going, keep striving, and keep persisting. If you give up on something you really care about, you may end up quitting even close to the finish line.

FINAL THOUGHTS ON THE FOUR CAPITALS AND SUCCESS

Success is purpose and goal dependent; therefore, success differs from individual to individual. One person's success may be another person's starting point, so success is very relative. Success is not time bound but seasonal, depending on the goals at a given time, but fulfilment has no timer. So do not set a timer for yourself, even though your goals ought to be time bound. You need to understand the seasons of your goals so as not to race against time. So rather than pursue success, pursue fulfilment and success will come along as the inevitable by-product of your fulfilment. It will happen if you diligently pursue your mission, with passion and perseverance. However, you can aim at success but focus on the purpose, goals and process. Remember always that success is a by-product of purpose, vision, goals, action, dedication, focus, perseverance and discipline, so plan for it and act on it. Success is accomplishment of purpose that comes with peace and happiness. When your accomplishment does not come with peace and happiness, it is pseudo-success.

Goals can be accomplished, and success can be achieved without peace and genuine happiness. A thief can have a goal and a vision to steal so much and can accomplish that goal. Once the goal is accomplished, success can be said to have been achieved, but that success may not come with peace of mind, even though it may come with some happiness, that is what I call pseudo-success.

Remember the story of Pablo Escobar, El Patron, the Colombian Drug Lord who achieved great success in his chosen field and became incredibly wealthy. He was listed in the most coveted Forbes List of the World's Richest People of Wealthy Industrialist and Investors as the 7th richest man in the world in 1989. But, he witnessed untold suffering and lack of peace of mind dying a day after his 44th birthday after a drawn-out manhunt. Therefore, do not aim at success, instead, aim at the fulfilment in life through a focus on purpose, passion, process, and perseverance, and success will follow.

Success cannot be chased because the accomplishment of today's goal becomes the beginning of a new goal; success must therefore develop, and it normally does so as the unintended side effect of one's personal dedication to a cause greater than oneself or as the by-product of one's surrender to bringing meaning to others and making them happier. So, do not chase success, create fulfilment and success will develop. Often, it is not the big things that make us truly happy in life. I want you to listen to what your conscience commands you to do and go on to carry it out to the best of your ability if it will bring you peace and happiness. Then you will live to see that eventually success will follow you because you made a life by living for others

However, today's society makes it difficult to focus, it screams at us to respond to the competition all around us. Do not be influenced or led by the competition, instead be led by your purpose and passion. Our society is characterized by an emphasis on accomplishment or achievement, often the achievement of wealth and power. The world glorifies people who are wealthy, powerful or popular in a chosen field, irrespective of the motives or process of accomplishment. Many a time, value, process and dignity are vilified in favour of outcome and interest (Power, Wealth or Popularity). However, true success is defined by dignity, contribution, impact, usefulness, fulfilment, happiness, safety, love, and peace of mind.

Think big but realistic. Learn how to push through your fears, do not be allayed by contentment, strive to climb and achieve your biggest goals and aspirations. Thoughts and actions are key, whatever your mind can conceive and believe, you can achieve, but do not expect a harvest without sowing and cultivation. The key to success is not merely through effort, but through enthusiasm and perseverance. A positive attitude may not solve all your problems but will help you navigate the climb, but passion without purpose can be self-destructive. You need a direction and some amount of aggression, and when you have any of these or both, you may well become successful. Discipline and constituency produce excellence.

Believe in yourself and use your four Capitals, **Personal Capital, Human Capital, Social Capital, and Spiritual Capital**, to let success and fulfilment ensue.

Personal Capital: be self-aware, regulate yourself, control yourself. Know who you are and what works or does not work for you, take care of your physical body and appearance, understand your personality purpose, passion, talents, gifts and environment. Regulate yourself by striving to do what you ought to do and avoid what you ought to avoid and control yourself by checking how you are doing with your plans and taking the needed corrective and improvement actions.

Human Capital: *Your know-what, know-how and execution power.* Gifts and Talents are not enough, you need to turn your talents into abilities through education, training and skill development. You also need current knowledge and information to enable you to execute your vision and goals in a smart and timely manner. That is the difference between your personal capital and human capital, your talent is your personal capital, your abilities are your human capital. You need to develop human capital. Planning and Preparation are key, but execution is paramount.

Social Capital: *be* deliberate about your relationships and networks. Your connections will speak and act for you when your personality and know-what cannot serve you.

Spiritual Capital: what helps you to stay focused on what you are fighting for. It works where all the others fail. It defines your adversity quotient and level of perseverance.

Let the Four Capitals for Success speak and work for you and you will be unstoppable with success and fulfilment. Your time is limited, so do not waste it chasing other people's aspirations. Create your vision and invest your four capitals in yourself by living to serve others and success will follow you. True wealth is the impact that yields fulfilment.

NOTE: Use the tool in Appendices A - H to assess your strengths, talents, passion and adversity quotient to develop your personal action plans.

BIBLIOGRAPHY

1. Bar-On, R. (2006). The Bar-On model of emotional-social intelligence (ESI). *Psicothema, 18(S)*, pp.13-25.
2. Bar-On, R. (2013). *Theoretical foundations, background and development of the Bar-On model of emotional intelligence.* Retrieved from http://www.reuvenbaron.org/wp/theoretical-foundations-background-and-development-of-the-bar-on-model-of-emotional-intelligence/
3. Bar-On, R., Tranel, D., Denburg, N. L., & Bechara, A. (2003). Exploring the neurological substrate of emotional and social intelligence. *Brain, 126(8)*, pp.1790-1800.
4. Bechara, A., Tranel, D., & Damasio, H. (2000). Characterization of the decision-making deficit of patients with ventromedial prefrontal cortex lesions. *Brain, 123(11)*, pp.2189-2202.
5. Boren, A. (2010). Emotional Intelligence: The secret of successful entrepreneurship? *Leadership in Agriculture, 2*, pp.55-61.
6. Brackett, M. A., & Salovey, P. (2006). Measuring emotional intelligence with the Mayer-Salovey-Caruso Emotional Intelligence Test (MSCEIT). *Psicothema, 18(S)*, pp.34-41.
7. Bradberry, T., & Greaves, J. (2009). *Emotional Intelligence 2.0.* TalentSmart.
8. Chee, M., & Choong, P. (2014). Social Capital, Emotional Intelligence and Happiness: An Investigation of the Asymmetric Impact of Emotional Intelligence on Happiness. *Academy of Educational Leadership Journal, 18(1)*, 105-116.
9. Dictionary.APA.org. (2018). *APA Dictionary of Psychology.* Retrieved from https://dictionary.apa.org/emotional-intelligence
10. Fiori, M., & Vesely-Maillefer, A. K. (2018). Emotional intelligence as an ability: theory, challenges, and new directions. In K. V. Keefer, J.

D. A. Parker, & D. H. Saklofske (Editors), *Emotional Intelligence in Education* (pp. 23-47). New York: Springer.

11. Goleman, D. (1995). *Emotional intelligence.* New York: Bantam Books.

12. Goleman, D. (1996). *Emotional Intelligence: why it can matter more than IQ.* London: Bloomsbury.

13. Goleman, D. (1998). *Working with emotional intelligence.* London: Bloomsbury.

14. Gopalan, S. (2016). *Creativity and Creative Thinking: World-Renowned Entrepreneurs, Professors* and *Psychologists Share Their Thoughts on Emotional Intelligence.* [Audiobook] Hachette Audio.

15. Gottman, J. M., & DeClaire, J. (1997). *Raising an **emotionally intelligent child**: The heart of parenting.* New York, NY: Simon & Schuster.

16. IFVS. (2018). Emotional intelligence: Skill building.

17. Malouff, J. M., Schutte, N. S., & Thorsteinsson, E. B. (2014). Trait emotional intelligence and romantic relationship satisfaction: A meta-analysis. *The American Journal of Family Therapy*, 42(1), pp.53-66.

18. Mayer, J., & Salovey, P. (1997). What is Emotional Intelligence? In P. Salovey and D. Sluyter (Eds). *Emotional Development and Emotional Intelligence.* New York: Basic Books.

19. Mayer, J. D., Salovey, P., & Caruso, D. (2002). *Mayer-Salovey-Caruso Emotional Intelligence Test manual.* Toronto: Multi-Health Systems.

20. Mayer, J. D., Salovey, P., & Caruso, D. R. (2005). *The Mayer–Salovey–Caruso Emotional Intelligence Test – Youth Version (MSCEIT-YV), Research Version.* Toronto: Multi Health Systems.

21. McCleskey, J. (2014). Emotional intelligence and leadership: A review of the progress, controversy, and criticism. *International Journal of Organizational Analysis*, 22(1), pp.76-93.

22. Papadogiannis, P. K., Logan, D., & Sitarenios, G. (2009). An ability model of emotional intelligence: A rationale, description, and application of the Mayer Salovey Caruso Emotional Intelligence Test (MSCEIT). In C. Stough, D. H. Saklofske, & J. D. A. Parker (editors), *Assessing emotional intelligence: Theory, Research, and applications (pp. 9-40).* New York: Springer.

23. Price, C., and Walle, E. (2018). *Sample MSCEIT Items.* Emotion Researcher. ISRE's Sourcebook for Research on Emotion and

Affect, Carolyn Price and Eric Walle (Eds.). Retrieved from http://emotionresearcher.com/wp-ontent/uploads/2015/03/SampleMSCEITItems.doc

24. Reece, R. (2018). *Emotional Intelligence & Conflict Management*. Retrieved from http://emotionalintelligenceworkshops.com/emotional-intelligence-conflict-management.htm

25. Salovey, P., & Grewal, D. (2005). The science of emotional intelligence. *Current directions in psychological science, 14(6)*, pp.281-285.

26. Schutte, N. S., Malouff, J. M., Bobik, C., Coston, T. D., Greeson, C., Jedlicka, C., & Wendorf, G. (2001). Emotional intelligence and interpersonal relations. *The Journal of social psychology, 141(4)*, pp. 523-536.

27. Spielberger, C. (2004). *Encyclopedia of applied psychology*. Boston: Academic Press.

28. TalentSmart.com. (2018). *A Life-Changing, True Story Reveals the Secret to Success*. Retrieved from http://www.talentsmart.com/articles/Life-Changing-True-Story-Reveals-the-Secret-to-Success-526472545-p-1.html

29. Therapistaid.com. (2018). *Triggers*. Retrieved from https://www.therapistaid.com/therapy-worksheet/triggers/emotions/none

30. Thompson, P. (2018). *9 Tips To Increase Your Emotional Intelligence For Stronger Relationships*. Retrieved from https://www.mindbodygreen.com/0-17573/9-tips-to-increase-your-emotional-intelligence-for-stronger-relationships.html.

APPENDIX A

Introduction.

I have developed a guide to help people take charge and plan their own personal development; I share it with you in table 4.2. The purpose of this personal development questionnaire is to help you plan your life, education, or career. I believe that life is a journey of learning and accomplishments and that the joy of learning comes not so much from what is learned, but from the process of learning and the outcomes of learning – where life itself is the greatest teacher and the achievement of purpose the outcome. This instrument is intended to help you find meaning in your life.

As you use this instrument, consider your lessons thoughtfully. I wish you success and great joy as you take responsibility for your career and personal development now. Remember, finding meaning in life comes from fulfilling your mission in life, from your accomplishments, and from appreciating the impact you make with those accomplishments. It is therefore important to start carving out your life path by asking yourself what life expects from you and what you have to offer it. To help you succeed, I assure you that this instrument will provide a mirror for personal introspection and your record of achievement.

The following sections will take you through questions that will help you to reflect on yourself, identify how you can improve your life and have a greater impact, and what you need to do to be successful and improve your life or career.

If you have any questions or need any clarification, please don't hesitate to consult me (Prof. Goski by telephone at +233 246452798 or by e-mail at goski.alabi@laweh.edu.gh or goski.alabi@gmail.com.

Goski Personal Development Plan: Do Not Say I have a Dream, Say I have a Plan

Name:
Date of birth:
Place of birth:
Date of this Assessment:

Record of Professional and Academic Achievements

My First Cycle Education Results (list grades and subjects):
My Secondary Level Results:
My A-level results:

My HND/ Associate Degree results:

My college, diploma, or university results:

Diploma:

Bachelor's:

Master's:

Doctorate (academic):

Doctorate (honorary):

Post doctorate (research):

Professional qualifications:

Academic rank:

Other:

Awards:

My Favourite Subjects

List your favourite subjects/courses:

List other professional development or training you are undertaking or have undertaken in the last year:

....

What books or subject matter do you like to read about beside your qualification(s) or professional area:

....

My Key Strengths

List your four key strengths:

- Calculation

- Reading

- Science

- Language

- Putting things together

- Bringing people together for a purpose

- Speaking

- Designing things

- Starting new businesses

- Managing and sustaining initiatives

- Entrepreneurship

- Helping others

- Resolving conflicts among people

- Being an advocate

- Encouraging others

- Other:

My Current Profession and Position at My Work or School

I am the/a:

- founder

- CEO

- shareholder

- manager

- supervisor

- team leader

- marketer

- lawyer

- practicing scientist

- technologist

- engineer

- public officer

- senior member

- civil servant

- junior staff

- prefect

- student

- worker

- president or an executive of an association(s) (name them)

- other(s)

My Past Career Aspirations

I have always dreamt of becoming:

I now want to become:

List your career aspirations in order of preference:

-
-
-

What changed your dream and why?

My Dream Career

I want to be a

....

My Current Profession or Academic or School Program

I trained / am training in:

My qualifications are:

Why I chose this profession:

My Current Occupation

Skip this section if you are not working but indicate that you are not working at the moment.

My current occupation is: For a living, I do this (describe what you are doing now in precise terms):

My Achievements

Imagine that you have to give an account of your life. What are the four key achievements of which you are most proud? List and describe them.   1.   2.   3.   4.

My Accomplishments

On a scale of 1 to 100, how do you rate your accomplishments so far?
Why?

Locating My Passion and Purpose

People always tell me I am good at............

I feel very fulfilled anytime I ....

I have a talent for ....

I am doing what I love most, and I make or want to make a living from that. Yes/No

My occupation is:

Does your occupation match your talent and interests?

I am working with my qualification or skills Yes/No ....

I aspire to be ....

What is the difference between your occupation, your talent, skills and your career or what you aspire to?

Does what you aspire to be match your interest and talents?

My Mission and Purpose in Life

I exist to..

I would like to be remembered for...

I am unique because...

My Future Career Aspirations

List three things you would like to do in the next five years in order or priority:

1.

2.

3.

Five years from now, I specifically see myself:

My Capabilities and Tendencies

Except for question 1 and 2, score yourself on a scale of 0 to 5, where 0 is none, 1 is low, and 5 is very high.

1. People admire me for:
2. I value experiences where I am able to.
3. I play by the rules.
4. I think first before acting.
5. I am spontaneous.
6. I think on my feet.
7. I take time to think or explore before responding to issues.
8. I am very focused.
9. I do many things at the same time.
10. I am tolerant of others.
11. I plan my time.
12. I set goals for myself and work toward them.
13. I work well under pressure:
14. I make a lot of effort in what I do.
15. I believe I can do anything I set my mind to.
16. I enjoy working alone.
17. I like taking risks.
18. I like myself.
19. I believe in myself.
20. I move around at work.
21. I can work with my hands.
22. I like to work outdoors.
23. I am always around many people.
24. I talk to people.
25. I listen to people.
26. I link people up and network.
27. I structure my own work.
28. I demonstrate expertise in an area.

29. I contribute new ideas or create new initiatives.

30. I answer complex questions.

31. I write and present my ideas.

32. I express my opinions freely.

33. I create and develop new things or ideas.

34. I help others through my work.

35. I contribute to a better world.

36. I make a difference.

37. I participate in personal development activities.

38. I work with others for a common purpose.

39. I get ahead in my career.

40. I influence others.

41. I afford a very comfortable lifestyle.

42. I attend to details to meet requirements.

43. I work in a secure environment.

44. I complete tasks that are clear and direct.

45. I predict my hours of work.

Interpretation of the Results of Your Self Ratings

If you scored yourself 4 or 5 on each question, it could also mean:

1. I play by the rules. *You are rigid.*
2. I think first before acting. *You are not flexible.*
3. I am spontaneous. *You are not focused and may not follow through.*
4. I think on my feet. *You are responsive.*
5. I take time to think or explore before responding to issues. *You're indecisive.*
6. I am very focused. *You can't see the big picture.*
7. I do many things at the same time. *You're easily distracted.*
8. I am tolerant of others. *You lack confidence.*
9. I plan my time. *You're not adaptable.*
10. I set goals for myself and work at them. *You're obsessive-compulsive.*
11. I work well under pressure. *You're bad at time management.*

12. I make a lot of effort in what I do. *You have no balance in work and life.*
13. I believe I can do anything I set my mind to. *You are arrogant.*
14. I enjoy working alone. *You do not play well with others.*
15. I like taking risks. *You are a thrill seeker.*
16. I like myself. *You are a narcissist.*
17. I believe very much in myself. *You are foolish.*
18. I move around at work. *You're a change agent.*
19. I like to work with my hands. *You are a doer and love to be involved.*
20. I like to work outdoors. *You're not an office person.*
21. I am always around many people. *You could become a politician, teacher, or pastor.*
22. I like to talk to people. *You could work in the media or as a pastor or counsellor.*
23. I listen to people. *You could become a counselor.*
24. I link people up and network. *You are connective.*
25. I structure my own work. *You are an entrepreneur.*
26. I demonstrate expertise in an area. *You could be a technocrat.*
27. I contribute new ideas or create new initiatives. *You are an innovator.*
28. I answer complex questions. *You could be a researcher/scientist.*
29. I write and present my ideas. *You could be a designer or innovator.*
30. I express my opinions freely. *You could be a politician.*
31. I create and develop new things or ideas. *You could be an engineer.*
32. I help others through my work. *You could be a caregiver, doctor, nurse, counsellor, or teacher.*
33. I contribute to a better world. *You could be a philanthropist or social worker.*
34. I like to make a difference. *You could be an artist, musician, or social scientist.*
35. I participate in personal development activities. *You are a narcissist.*
36. I work with others for a common purpose. *You are a team player.*
37. I get ahead in my career. *You are competitive.*
38. I influence others. *You could be a politician or psychologist.*
39. I afford a very comfortable lifestyle. *You could be a businessperson.*
40. I attend to details to meet requirements. *You could be a technocrat or a quality-assurance officer or work in law enforcement.*

41. I work in a secure environment. *You could be a white-collar worker.*
42. I complete tasks that are clear and direct. *You are not flexible, you work to rule, or you are a conformist. You could be an office worker.*
43. I Predict my hours of work. *You commit to different engagements*

Preparing for My Career Goal(s)

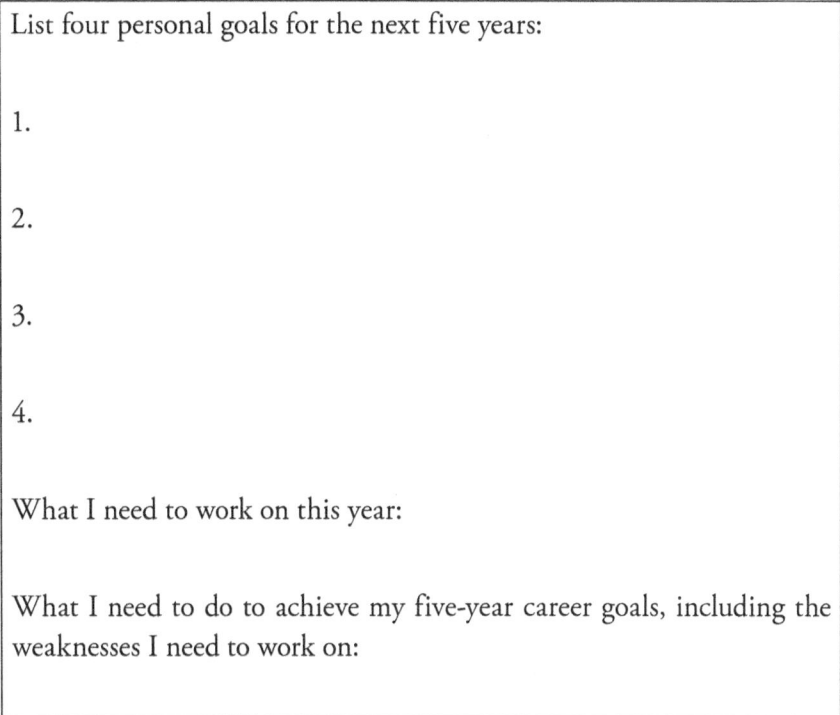

List four personal goals for the next five years:

1.

2.

3.

4.

What I need to work on this year:

What I need to do to achieve my five-year career goals, including the weaknesses I need to work on:

My Personal Action Matrix

Personal action plans are road maps for achieving success. The aim of a Personal Action Plan is to develop a plan of action for your future, which helps to identify key goals, steps, possible challenges and things to take care of to achieve personal success. Milestones describe the major progress points that must be reached to achieve success.

Describe the activities you must undertake to accomplish goals, one after the other in the activities' column, indicate when you have to accomplish it, where it has to be done, name the people needed to help you accomplish those activities or milestones and the kind of support you need from them. Then indicate what will show that you have accomplished that activity or milestone. Repeat this for all the goals you have set for yourself. Encourage yourself to follow through your activities and milestones. Make it a point to dedicate an hour or two to these activities each day. Indicate what can go wrong or undermine your ability to achieve that goal.

My Five-Year Vision and Plan

My Mission and Purpose in Life is to: ....

My Vision: To be a ....five years from now.

My Key Goals (identify just four)

- Goal 1:
- Goal 2:
- Goal 3:
- Goal 4:

Goal 1: (Restate Goal 1 here)

Activities:	When?	Where?	Who?	What support?	How to measure?
Milestone:					
What can go wrong, and what will you do in such an event?					

Goal 2: Restate the Goal Here

Activities:	When?	Where?	Who?	What support?	How to measure?
Milestone:					
What can go wrong, and what will you do in such an event?					

Goal 3: Restate the Goal

Activities	When?	Where?	Who?	What support?	How to measure?
Milestone:					
What can go wrong, and what will you do in such an event?					

Goal 4

Activities	When?	Where?	Who?	What support?	How do I know I have achieved it?
Milestone:					
What can go wrong, and what will you do in such an event?					

My Monthly Plan

Month	Activity	Remarks
January		
February		
March		
April		
May		
June		
July		
August		
September		
October		
November		
December		

My Weekly Planner

I plan my week: Yes/No (circle one)

I follow my weekly plans closely: Yes/No (circle one)

If I have to do a weekly planner, this is what it would look like:

	Sunday	Monday	Tuesday	Wednesday	Thursday	Friday	Saturday
6–7 a.m.							
7–8 a.m.							
8–9 a.m.							
9–10 a.m.							
10–11 a.m.							
11 a.m.–12 noon							
12 noon–1 p.m.							
1–2 p.m.							
2–3 p.m.							
4–5 p.m.							
5–6 p.m.							
6–7 p.m.							
7–8 p.m.							
8–9 p.m.							
9–10 p.m.							
Sleep							

Remember to incorporate some social activities into your weekly planner. All work and no play makes Jack or Jill a dull person, and all play and no work makes Jack or Jill a fool.

Remember to include "thinking time" in your planner.

My Fun Activities

I enjoy the following activities:

- Chess

- Computer Games

- Monopoly

- Scrabble

- Football

- Basketball

- Religious meetings

- Dance

- Yoga

- Volunteering at Community activities

- Using social media purposefully

- Environment improvement

- Advocacy

- Other

My Research Guide

My favourite research sites are:

My sanctuary is:

My favourite blogs are:

Personalities I follow are:

My Critical Support Group: List the people you consult when you have concerns with the different aspects of life as indicated below

These are the people who can help you implement your ideas. They must be selected carefully, complement each other, have great relational skills, and be tech-savvy. They should be people you like and can learn from and relate with well. Also, they should be people you believe you can work with. Trust your hunches as much as possible.

List the people and indicate for each person how you believe they can be of help:

I consult with this person when I have concerns about:

Financial issues:

Family issues:

Career issues:

Business ideas:

Relationships:

Spiritual issues:

Encouragement:

Public relations:

Unwind:

Crisis:

These are the people who can help you accomplish your goals and develop. They should be people you trust and believe are stronger than you in certain areas. They should be people you like and can relate to well. Remember to choose people who can complement your strengths and weaknesses. Make it a point to meet with each of these people at least once a year.

My Useful Links

My useful links include:

Additional Notes

Any thoughts:

Take a Personality Test (Myers–Briggs, PSA, StrengthsFinder, etc.)

The personality test will enable you to understand yourself and others around you. The test will help you know your best self, enhance self-confidence, build stronger relationships, and progress your career. Take a test using any available instrument. Visit the link below for a free personality test.

https://www.16personalities.com/free-personality-test

Visit the link below to find your strengths: https://high5test.com/

Self-Control: Progress Review

Review of Personal Achievement
What went well?
What did not go well and why?
What could you have done better?
Has there been any change to your personal plans?
What could have been improved upon?

www.ingramcontent.com/pod-product-compliance
Lightning Source LLC
Chambersburg PA
CBHW021407210526
45463CB00001B/249